Cambridge Elements ≡

Elements in Global Urban History
edited by
Michael Goebel
Graduate Institute Geneva
Tracy Neumann
Wayne State University
Joseph Ben Prestel
Freie Universität Berlin

URBAN DISASTERS

Cindy Ermus
University of Texas at San Antonio

CAMBRIDGE
UNIVERSITY PRESS

Shaftesbury Road, Cambridge CB2 8EA, United Kingdom

One Liberty Plaza, 20th Floor, New York, NY 10006, USA

477 Williamstown Road, Port Melbourne, VIC 3207, Australia

314–321, 3rd Floor, Plot 3, Splendor Forum, Jasola District Centre, New Delhi – 110025, India

103 Penang Road, #05–06/07, Visioncrest Commercial, Singapore 238467

Cambridge University Press is part of Cambridge University Press & Assessment, a department of the University of Cambridge.

We share the University's mission to contribute to society through the pursuit of education, learning and research at the highest international levels of excellence.

www.cambridge.org
Information on this title: www.cambridge.org/9781009001908

DOI: 10.1017/9781009004053

ISBN 978-1-009-00190-8 Paperback
ISSN 2632-3206 (online)
ISSN 2632-3192 (print)

Urban Disasters

Elements in Global Urban History

DOI: 10.1017/9781009004053
First published online: July 2023

Cindy Ermus
University of Texas at San Antonio

Author for correspondence: Cindy Ermus, Cindy.ermus@utsa.edu

Abstract: This Element explores the history of urban disasters around the globe over the past 300 years. It introduces the reader to central concepts that help define the study of disasters, then moves on to explore the relationship between cities and disasters, including earthquakes, hurricanes, fires, and epidemics. It asks, for example: How have cities responded in times of crisis, and what practices, infrastructures, and/or institutions have they introduced to prevent disasters from reoccurring? Who suffers most when urban disasters strike, and why? In what ways do catastrophes change cities? How, if at all, are cities unique from the countryside? To answer these questions and more, this concise history looks at a series of case studies from the eighteenth century through the COVID-19 pandemic. The Element concludes with a brief look at the ongoing effects of climate change and the future of cities.

Keywords: cities, urban history, disasters, environment, public health

ISBNs: 9781009001908 (PB), 9781009004053 (OC)
ISSNs: 2632-3206 (online), 2632-3192 (print)

Contents

1 Introduction: Defining Disaster

On December 26, 2004, roughly 30 kilometers (19 miles) beneath the ocean floor, a massive rupture took place along the India and Burma Plates (parts of the Indo-Australian and Eurasian Plates, respectively) about 160 kilometers (99 miles) off the northern coast of the Indonesian island of Sumatra. Within fifteen minutes, mega-tsunami waves unleashed by the 9.1-magnitude earthquake began arriving on the coasts of Sumatra's Aceh Province.[1] Over the next many hours, the colossal waves would strike along the coasts of fifteen countries and trigger the transformation of urban, coastal, and political landscapes across the Indian Ocean.[2]

The 2004 Indian Ocean Tsunami (also known as the Asian Tsunami, Sumatra Tsunami, Boxing Day Tsunami, and the Sumatra-Andaman Earthquake) unfolded over a period of hours. Yet the temblor below the ocean did not mark the beginning, nor did receding waters mark the end, of this expansive, historic catastrophe. Approximately a quarter of a million lives were lost (though, as is typical with catastrophes of this scale, we may never know the exact number). In Aceh Province alone, 35,000 children were orphaned, and many of these were soon preyed upon by human traffickers.[3] As many as 1.7 million people were displaced as the sea swallowed entire villages.[4] The saltwater damaged tens of thousands of hectares of agricultural land, while vegetation up to hundreds of meters inland disappeared in an instant. The human and financial cost of the catastrophe was staggering, and in many ways, the damage endures. Many years later, those who experienced or were affected by the calamity continue to grapple with their trauma, struggling with post-traumatic stress disorder (PTSD), depression, and/or anxiety.[5]

Disasters are not acute occurrences. They do not end when the earth has stopped shaking nor when a hurricane has moved back out to sea. For starters, the factors and mechanisms that can create conditions for a disaster to unfold are in place long before the actual hazard arrives, be it an earthquake, a big storm, a fire, a flood, a tornado, or any other force, natural or otherwise. Moreover, ramifications of disaster – for the environment, society, and the individual – can remain long after the smoke has cleared. These may include damage to the urban built environment and infrastructure, environmental degradation,

---

[1] Karan, "Introduction," 7.

[2] These were Indonesia, Sri Lanka, India, Thailand, Somalia, Myanmar, Maldives, Malaysia, Tanzania, Seychelles, Bangladesh, South Africa, Yemen, Kenya, and Madagascar. See Juran, "Indian Ocean Tsunami, 2004," 198.

[3] Jasparro and Taylor, "Transnational Geopolitical Competition and Natural Disasters," 289.

[4] Schreurs, "Improving Governance Structures for Natural Disaster Response," 261.

[5] See, for example, Frankenberg and colleagues, "Mental Health in Sumatra after the Tsunami"; Kar, Krishnaraaj, and Rameshraj, "Long-Term Mental Health Outcomes."

political conflict or instability, the threat of epidemic disease, displacement, destitution, or trauma. Rather than signify an extreme event that is over in seconds, minutes, or hours, disasters instead represent long processes, with a beginning that predates their unfolding and an end that is seldom easy to locate. As historian Andy Horowitz has observed, "Their causes and consequences stretch across much longer periods of time and space than we commonly imagine."[6]

Disasters are also great revealers. As I have noted elsewhere, calamitous events lay bare the strengths or weaknesses in a state; they expose underlying power structures, political interests, economic and diplomatic concerns, social divisions and tensions, as well as who among the populace is most valued, and, conversely, who is deemed disposable and thus rendered more vulnerable to potentially dangerous hazards by targeted structural inequities.[7] Although this can be true in both rural and urban catastrophes, as well as environmental ones (consider major oil spills, for example), disasters are especially revealing when they occur in cities where most of the earth's population now lives. Today, roughly 55 percent of the global population, equivalent to about 4.2 billion people, lives in urban areas. By 2030, this number is expected to grow to 60 percent; one out of every three people will live in cities with at least half a million inhabitants.[8] Densely populated, diverse, industrial, and built up, cities are microcosms of the global order. For centuries, people have been attracted to what they have to offer: opportunities for employment and education, trade and commerce, access to resources such as hospitals and schools, as well as the conveniences of retail, entertainment, airports, and so on. Yet many, especially our most populated coastal urban areas, have become capitals of vulnerability.

Although cities are not necessarily more vulnerable to natural hazards than rural areas – in fact, analyses on earthquake-related casualties have found that in some parts of the world, rural communities suffer disproportionately – a hazard's effects are likely to be catastrophic on a grander scale.[9] The industry, built environment, and larger concentration of inhabitants in cities mean that

---

[6] Horowitz, *Katrina*, 3.   [7] Ermus, *The Great Plague Scare of 1720*, 217–18.

[8] United Nations Department of Social and Economic Affairs, *The World's Cities in 2018*.

[9] See Wyss, "Disadvantage of the Rural"; Weber, "Rural Areas May Suffer Disproportionately in Quakes"; Hewitt, *Regions of Risk*, 218. See also Oven and Bankoff, "The Neglected Country(side)." Writing about earthquakes, geographer Kenneth Hewitt too has noted, "The worst catastrophes are generally those in which severe shaking affects large, densely occupied urban areas. However, this is less frequent than disasters affecting rural and small settlements, partly because these involve much larger areas within earthquake-prone regions." Hewitt, *Regions of Risk*, 197. One hazard to which urban areas are more uniquely vulnerable than the countryside is extreme heat (or heat waves). Whereas natural landscapes can absorb the sun's heat, the urban built environment – including buildings, roads, sidewalks, and so forth – reflects it, causing what is known as the heat island effect.

any major disturbance could be costlier and affect more people. An urban disaster is also more likely to affect regions far beyond the city limits. Many urban areas are home to critical infrastructures, manufacturing plants, and/or commercial ports on which disparate parts of the world rely. Significant interruptions can therefore have major implications for daily life across the globe, affecting, for example, regional or global economies or the global supply chain (the price and availability of certain items).[10] These factors are part of the reason urban disasters garner so much more attention in the media than rural disasters, which in turn results in rural areas having less access to the resources necessary to increase resilience. Not attracting the eyes of the world means less aid and personnel, less financial support, and therefore a diminished ability to make necessary changes to laws and building regulations.

Still, cities are cast with unique vulnerabilities. On October 31, 2018, designated World Cities Day by the United Nations, the Department of Economic and Social Affairs (UN DESA) reported that the majority of the world's cities are vulnerable to at least one type of hazard, including earthquakes, cyclones, floods, droughts, landslides, and volcanic eruptions.[11] And at least partly as a result of anthropogenic (human-caused) climate change, as well as human activity such as the destruction of natural storm barriers (for example, mangrove forests), the paving over of floodplains (which increases surface runoff and therefore flood risk), and other forms of human encroachment, such hazards are more frequently resulting in disasters. Between 1970 and 2019, the number of catastrophes resulting from extreme weather events jumped fivefold, accounting for 50 percent of disasters across the globe, 45 percent of all reported deaths (91 percent of which occurred in developing countries), and 74 percent of all reported economic losses.[12] This increase in the frequency and intensity of extreme events, combined with the exposure and lack of preparedness of communities around the globe, has resulted in what I call the "new disaster realities" of our era, in which we are forced to reckon with the consequences of humanity's exploitations. Many of the world's largest, most densely populated cities, moreover, are situated along coastlines, which exposes them to hazards from which inland settlements are mostly shielded: cyclones and coastal storms, tsunamis, and, increasingly, the slow disaster of rising seas resulting from anthropogenic climate change. Today, it is worth noting, roughly 10 percent of the global population lives in a low-elevation coastal zone (less than 10

---

[10] Rural disasters too can destroy important crops, livestock, and so forth, with similarly important implications for the price and availability of goods around the globe, yet urban disasters nevertheless garner more attention in the media.

[11] Ibid., 9.

[12] United Nations, "Climate and Weather-Related Disasters Surge Five-Fold over 50 Years."

meters of elevation), even though this represents only 2.2 percent of the earth's land surface,[13] and about 40 percent (more than 2.5 billion people) live within 100 kilometers (62 miles) of the coast.[14] In fact, coastal metropolises – such as Tokyo, Mumbai, Osaka, New York, Buenos Aires, and many, many others – are home to a majority of the world's urban population (roughly 53 percent).[15]

The importance of cities and urban vulnerabilities in discussions about disaster, then, cannot be overstated, hence the purpose of the present Element. By looking at a series of case studies from around the world, this concise history examines how cities have experienced urban disasters, including earthquakes, tsunamis, cyclones and floods, fires, and disease epidemics. It is intended as an introduction to the subject of urban disasters that explores many of the central concepts and ideas that help define their study, as well as the role of human decisions in the process of disaster-making. Some of the questions it seeks to answer include: Why do disasters happen? What is the relationship between cities and disaster? How have cities responded in times of crisis, and what kind of practices, infrastructures, and/or institutions have urban areas introduced to prevent disasters? Relatedly, in what ways have catastrophes served to change cities in the long term? Perhaps most importantly, what does this all mean for us today as the cities of the world face the ongoing effects of climate change? This Element will explore the effects of disasters on urban populations, infrastructures, laws, building regulations, public health policies, and a number of other elements over the past 300 years. In the end, the reader will find that urban disasters are a complex marriage of destruction and renewal, of failures and opportunities, of winners and losers.

Consistent with the nature of both urban and disaster history, this Element is informed by scholarship from across disciplines. The study of disasters, like the study of cities, is fundamentally and necessarily interdisciplinary. Disaster history borrows and benefits from findings and perspectives in a host of other disciplines and fields that unite to provide a fuller understanding of the countless complex factors that contribute to a disaster's unfolding. Disaster history also benefits from a global or transnational approach that considers the broader effects and implications of a disaster across time and space and allows for comparisons from which we can draw lessons for the present. Disasters, after all, are always with us: on our newsfeeds, on our televisions, in our literature, perhaps in our region or neighborhood, in our past, and in our future. In this era

---

[13] United Nations, "Ocean Conference Fact Sheet"; McGranahan, Balk, and Anderson, "Low Coastal Zone Settlements," 16.

[14] United Nations, "Ocean Conference Fact Sheet."

[15] Barragán and Andrés, "Analysis and Trends of the World's Coastal Cities and Agglomerations," 12–13.

of climate change, extreme weather, disease, and general unrest, we need lessons from the past perhaps more than ever. This Element is one small contribution to the cause.

1.1 Central Concepts and Terminology

Beyond the scope of the present paragraph, I do not employ the phrase "natural disaster" anywhere in this Element, and the reason is simple: *natural* disasters do not exist. The term "natural disaster," which denotes an "act of God" or an adverse event that occurs through natural processes – which is to say, beyond human influence or control – is, at best, problematic. The very origins of the word "disaster" itself – from Greek and Latin terms for "bad star" or "ill-starred event" – point to this understanding of disasters as natural occurrences beyond our control. Consequently, the label of "natural disaster" removes, too often deliberately, all responsibility from human actors and their decisions in creating a disaster, when in fact, the human element is central, if to varying degrees. Consider, for example, a hurricane. The characteristics that define a hurricane – a rotating storm with strong winds, rain, a low-pressure center, and so forth – are not, in themselves, synonymous with "disaster." While at sea, in other words, a hurricane is little more than a big storm.[16] The *disaster* results when this large, rotating system approaches a coastline made vulnerable by factors such as coastline development and large populations, inadequate flood and/or wind infrastructure, lack of storm barriers (natural or otherwise), construction in low-lying areas, and so on. Put another way, although a hurricane itself is not human made (even if these storms *are* becoming stronger and more frequent as a result of anthropogenic climate change), its development into a disaster will result not merely from its movement inland but, largely, from human decisions made on the ground for decades or even centuries before its arrival. In place of "natural disaster," then, I use "hazard," "natural hazard,"[17] or "extreme event" to refer to a naturally occurring event – such as a big storm, earthquake, or volcanic eruption – that can trigger widespread damage among a population rendered vulnerable by human-driven factors and decisions.[18]

---

[16] Oliver-Smith, "Introduction," 7.

[17] The United Nations Office for Disaster Risk Reduction (UNDRR) defines "hazard" as a "process, phenomenon or human activity that may cause loss of life, injury or other health impacts, property damage, social and economic disruption or environmental degradation ... Natural hazards are predominantly associated with natural processes and phenomena." United Nations Office for Disaster Risk Reduction, "Terminology."

[18] One could also argue, as disaster and health scholar Ilan Kelman has, that the phrase "natural hazard," used in this Element to refer to these naturally occurring phenomena, is also problematic for reasons similar to those just listed, which is to say, there is no such thing as a natural hazard. A natural event, like a hurricane (to use the same example), is not in and of itself any

What, then, does it mean to be vulnerable? What *is* vulnerability, and what, in turn, does it mean to be resilient? In some ways, these two central concepts go hand in hand. In the context of disaster studies, vulnerability – from the Latin *vulnerabilis*, meaning to wound or injure – refers to the conditions or circumstances in place that increase the exposure and/or susceptibility of a community, society, system, or an individual to the detrimental effects of a hazard. These conditions can be shaped by physical, social, economic, and/or environmental factors – for example, colonialism, capitalism, white supremacy, gender, religion, age, disability, and so on – and they determine the extent to which a natural event, like a hurricane or an earthquake, becomes a disaster.[19] Vulnerability, in other words, does not merely exist but is constructed. Meanwhile, resilience – from the Latin *resilire*, which means to rebound or spring back – refers to the capacity of a person, system, community, or society to resist, absorb, adapt to, or recover from the effects of a hazard.[20] It too is constructed, more often than not, to the benefit of the wealthy and advantaged. Vulnerability thus signifies a lack or absence of resilience, and vice versa. It is important to note, as Bavel and colleagues have, that "Determinants of vulnerability, although situationally specific, often incorporate various aspects of distribution of wealth, resources, support, and opportunity, while resilience is determined to a significant extent by social, economic, and political institutions and the context in which they function."[21] In effect, this results in urban landscapes that comprise various levels of vulnerability. A single city can have areas that are considered resilient to a particular hazard, and others that are vulnerable to various degrees. The more resilient neighborhoods are likely to be whiter and more affluent, while more vulnerable areas tend to be home to racial and ethnic minorities and to households of lower socioeconomic status (SES). These, in turn, may be marked by shoddier construction and/or be built in low-lying areas or otherwise less desirable geographic locations. In this context, it is useful to introduce the concept of risk. Risk, we can say, is "'a product of three major elements: exposure to hazards ..., the frequency or severity of the hazard, and the vulnerability.' More precisely, it is the likely level of loss from a given magnitude of hazard combined with the potential for harm."[22] And this potential for harm, this *risk*, is not evenly distributed. Instead, like resilience, it is determined

---

more a *hazard* than it is a disaster, unless we – humans – make it so. Kelman, *Disaster by Choice*, 40; Kelman, "Natural Disasters Do Not Exist," 3.

[19] United Nations Office for Disaster Risk Reduction, "Terminology."

[20] Ibid. The introduction to Remes and Horowitz's volume *Critical Disaster Studies* includes a valuable discussion on the terms introduced here and the extent to which they are, essentially, political. See Horowitz and Remes, "Introduction," 1–8.

[21] Bavel et al., *Disasters and History*, 24.

[22] Birkmann, "Risk and Vulnerability Indicators," 21; Modica and Zoboli, "Vulnerability," 61.

to a large degree by political, economic, and social motivations that, through the decisions of human actors, can influence the level of risk a particular area is exposed to in the face of a hazard.

Hazards, vulnerability, risk, resilience – these are some of the more central concepts mentioned throughout this Element. I would also like to draw attention to my use of perhaps the most central terms in this Element: "urban" and "disaster" (and, by extension, "catastrophe," "calamity," and "crisis"). By "urban" – from the Latin *urbs*, meaning city or large town – I mean in or related to a city, *including* the urban periphery, which is to say the settled areas extending from the city center (such as the suburbs). A city proper, by which I mean the urban area within official city limits, does not operate alone or exist in isolation. It functions in tandem with surrounding areas that provide a workforce, clientele, foods, materials, and other resources, and that often represent an extension of the city's identity. Based on these understandings, I use the terms "city," "urban area," and "urban center" interchangeably. The word "disaster," meanwhile, is typically understood as a sudden, overwhelming occurrence that causes extensive damage. In fact, the Oxford Dictionary defines it as "a sudden accident or natural catastrophe that causes great damage or loss of life," but, as we have already seen, this definition is problematic.[23] For one, there is no such thing as a "natural catastrophe," nor are disasters sudden occurrences. Instead, as I discussed earlier, disasters must be understood as long, drawn-out events with a history *and* a future. The United Nations Office for Disaster Risk Reduction (UNDRR) thus offers a more detailed definition of the term: "a serious disruption of the functioning of a community or a society involving widespread human, material, economic or environmental losses and impacts, which exceeds the ability of the affected community or society to cope using its own resources." The words "catastrophe" and "calamity" are defined in much the same way. Oxford defines the former as "an event causing great and usually sudden damage or suffering; a disaster," and the latter as "an event that causes great damage to people's lives, property, etc."[24] Finally, the word "crisis" comes to us from the Greek *krisis*, meaning either "decision," or as Hippocrates and Galen used it, "the turning point of a disease." Despite this medical origin, however, Oxford now defines it as "a time of intense difficulty or danger … when decisions must be made." Rather than a sudden and/or destructive event, it is, more broadly, a time of challenge or difficulty. Based on these understandings, this Element uses "disaster," "catastrophe," and "calamity" interchangeably, but uses "crisis" to refer more broadly to any significant time or instance of emergency.

---

[23] "Disaster, n." *OED Online*.

[24] "Catastrophe" comes to us from the Greek and Latin terms *katastrophē* and *catastropha*, respectively, which means "overturning" or "sudden turn," while the Latin *calamitatem* or *calamitas* refers to disaster, damage, or misfortune.

1.2 Structure of This Element

This Element is organized thematically. Each section looks at a different type of hazard, including earthquakes and tsunamis, storms and floods, urban fires, and disease epidemics. The Element then concludes with a brief look at climate change and at some of the ways in which it is changing our cities. While most urban histories *and* histories of disaster have focused on North America and Europe, the case studies considered here are situated all over the globe, including South and North America, the Caribbean, Europe, Africa, South Asia, East Asia, and Southeast Asia. An exploration of disasters in urban areas around the world offers grounds for comparison from which we can draw important lessons. Some of the regions discussed here not only encounter a higher number of disasters, but their experience of calamity can reveal alternative strategies for coping with or managing disasters across time and geographic space.[25] By looking at the history of urban disasters since the eighteenth century, this Element offers tools for understanding the present and encourages the reader to contemplate both the future of cities and the future of disasters.

2 Earthquakes and Tsunamis

Some catastrophes are so colossal and widespread that they are nearly incomprehensible. Time and again, such disasters of biblical proportions consist not of a single hazard, but of a combination, with one following the other in a domino effect. Not infrequently in the history of disasters, the initial natural hazard behind such cascading calamities is an earthquake. When the shaking of the earth unravels into a catastrophe upon an unprepared, vulnerable population, it can unleash a Pandora's box of misfortunes. It is a hazard that begets additional hazards, including fires, tsunamis, and/or disease epidemics, as well as longer-term crises, such as poverty and displacement (which can follow other types of hazards as well).

Among the most notorious historical examples of a catastrophe of this scale is the Lisbon Earthquake of 1755. At about 9:45 on the morning of November 1, 1755, the earth below the city of Lisbon and surrounding areas began to shake as people congregated in churches all over the region for All Saints' Day. The immediate effects of the temblor were devastating. Buildings crumbled, crushing many of the churchgoers and leaving thousands homeless. The megathrust earthquake, which originated roughly 200 kilometers (124 miles) off the coast of Cape St. Vincent, Portugal, then gave way to massive waves that crashed onto the coasts of Portugal, Spain, and Morocco, and parts of the West Indies and Brazil.[26]

---

[25] Ewen, *What Is Urban History?*, 89.

[26] Molesky, *This Gulf of Fire*, 19. The earthquake is estimated to have measured at least 8.5 on the moment magnitude scale (M_w), but was possibly above 9.1. See ibid., 6.

In Lisbon, it swept hundreds of victims out to sea, many of whom had congregated in open areas on the riverbank, where the royal palace and other important administrative buildings stood, to escape falling debris.[27] But the tragic spectacle was not yet over. Throughout the city, the tremors gave rise to hundreds of fires that combined to create a veritable firestorm that left much of the once bustling, densely populated city center in a heap of ashes.[28] Many thousands who had survived the earthquake and tsunami perished from the flames and fumes that overtook the city.[29] Of Lisbon's forty *freguesias* (civil parishes or subdivisions), all suffered extensive damage and many were completely destroyed.[30] As the smoke cleared, the British consul, Edward Hay, described the destruction near the riverfront:

> The part of the town towards the water where was the Royal Palace, the public tribunals, the Customs House, India House, and where most of the merchants dealt for the convenience of transacting their business, is so totally destroyed by the earthquake and by the fire, that it is nothing but a heap of rubbish, in many places several stories high.[31]

Ultimately, the triple disaster took as many as 43,000 lives in Portugal and shocked much of the contemporary world.[32]

To this day, the Lisbon Earthquake is credited with inspiring new ways of thinking about nature, disasters, and the environment, and stimulating advances in seismology and other aspects of geophysics. But how did it change the city? In many ways, the disaster of 1755 resulted in a new Lisbon. Prior to the earthquake, the ancient commercial capital – situated on the northern banks of the Tagus River (Rio Tejo) – retained its largely medieval layout. Narrow, uneven, meandering streets and alleyways stretched across the city, many strewn with rubbish and congested with vagrants.[33] The city's structures too bore little resemblance to those that would be erected in their place. Images of pre-1700s Lisbon depict a townscape medieval in its appearance, with structures packed tightly together, surrounded by a city wall, on the edge of the river (Figure 1).[34]

---

[27] Ibid., 6. This plaza is called the Terreiro do Paço or Praça do Comércio. The buildings it housed, including the royal palace (Paço da Ribeira), were destroyed during the disaster.

[28] Ibid., 7, 157. A firestorm occurs when a fire becomes so intense that it creates its own wind system.

[29] Penn et al., "The Pombaline Quarter of Lisbon," 3.

[30] Rodrigues and Craig, "Recovery amid Destruction," 399.   [31] As quoted in ibid.

[32] Molesky, *This Gulf of Fire*, 298.   [33] Ibid., 63.

[34] Braun, Georg, Or, Frans Hogenberg, P. Von Brachel, Anton Hierat, Abraham Hogenberg, Simon Novellanus, Joris Hoefnagel, Jacob Hoefnagel, Jacob Van Deventer, and Henrik Rantzau. "Lisbona." *Civitates Orbis Terrarvm* [*Coloniae Agrippinae: apud Petrum à Brachel, sumptibus auctorum, to 1618, 1612*]. Map of Lisbon. www.loc.gov/resource/g3200m.gct00128a/?sp=14. This version, on the Library of Congress website, allows the viewer to zoom in and observe the image with remarkable detail.

Figure 1 Detail of "Lisbona" in *Civitates Orbis Terrarvm* (Cities of the World)
by Georg Braun (1541–1622). Map of Lisbon. Library of Congress.
www.loc.gov/resource/g3200 m.gct00128a/?sp=14

By the first half of the eighteenth century, this wealthy commercial port's
architecture was more diverse than the antiquated city depicted in Figure 1,
featuring elements of Moorish, Romanesque, Gothic, Renaissance, and
Manueline architecture, among many others. The latter, a late Gothic style
named after Portuguese monarch Manuel I (r. 1495–1521), was itself
a composite architectural style characterized in part by elaborate maritime and
botanical motifs carved into stone doorways, columns, and windows.[35] Yet little
would remain of these original structures. Under the direction of the famous
Marquis of Pombal (Sebastião José de Carvalho e Melo, Marquês de Pombal
e Conde de Oeiras, 1699–1782), the chief minister of King Joseph I, Lisbon was
reconstructed upon secular and more empirical understandings of seismology
and the environment. The result was an earthquake-resistant, neoclassical
metropolis that is still visible in today's Baixa Pombalina neighborhood. At
this time, the number of churches in Lisbon was decreased, and in a move
somewhat reminiscent of the desacralization of France almost four decades later
during the height of the French Revolution, the names of important streets were
changed to direct emphasis away from church, crown, and nobility and, in this
case, toward the middle class.[36] Most notably, with an eye to addressing the very

---

[35] Molesky, *This Gulf of Fire*, 36.   [36] Ibid., 315.

vulnerabilities that helped give rise to the widespread destruction and great number of casualties, streets were now significantly widened and a number of large squares were constructed. The city was also divided into large blocks that could provide more stability during future earthquakes.[37] Structures were reinforced in the ground with flexible pine logs treated with salt to prevent both combustion and deterioration, and foundations now followed a north–south axis that designers thought would provide greater structural stability (since they believed the tremors had moved in that direction).[38] Perhaps the most impressive and effective technological and architectural innovation at this time was the *gaiola pombalina*, or pombaline cage – a masonry building reinforced with a skeleton of timber crosses. In the event of an earthquake, the timber frame would hold intact even if the masonry within gave way.[39] The *gaiola* represented a notable advance in architecture and earthquake-resistant technology, and many of these buildings, or *gaioleiros*, stand in Lisbon to this day.[40]

The city's vulnerability to fire was also a major concern in the aftermath of the disaster, and several measures were implemented to help prevent a similar inferno from reoccurring in the future. During the rebuilding of Lisbon, buildings had firebreak walls installed to inhibit a fire's movement between buildings; ground floors were constructed not of wood but of vaulted stone; fire pumps and leather buckets (for transporting water) were installed near the city's parish churches; and bakeries – believed to have been where many of the fires started after the earthquake – were clustered behind a high wall along the Calçada de São Francisco.[41]

The sheer magnitude and violence of the great Lisbon earthquake, tsunami, and fire of 1755, as well its effects – both short and long term – on the affected people, cities, and regions, and on the arts, literature, philosophy, and sciences (especially seismology) of the eighteenth century, have earned it a prominent place in the history of urban disasters. Although its influence on the intellectual movement known as the Enlightenment has at times been overblown, overshadowing important developments and disasters that took place earlier in the century, its importance in this history is clear.[42] Yet it does not stand alone. Many earthquakes of similarly epic proportions have wrought death and destruction across large regions both prior to 1755 and since. Consider the powerful San Francisco earthquake and fire of 1906. The 7.7-moment-magnitude (M_w) tremor lasted roughly one minute, then triggered devastating fires throughout the city.[43] Over three days, the blaze destroyed much of what

---

[37] Ibid., 313.   [38] Ibid., 315.   [39] Dan, "Timber Frame Historic Structures," 220.

[40] Azevedo, Serrano, and Oliveira, "The Next 1755," 564.

[41] Molesky, *This Gulf of Fire*, 316.   [42] See, for example, Ermus, "Managing Disaster."

[43] Steinberg, *Acts of God*, 27. As many as 3,000 people died from the earthquake and fire.

the earthquake had spared, but ultimately led to a city completely transformed. Consider too the Great Chilean Earthquake of 1960, the most powerful earthquake on record, measuring an astonishing 9.5 M_w – 350 times more powerful than the San Francisco Earthquake.[44] Also known as the Valdivia Earthquake and Tsunami, the disaster took hundreds of lives and left as many as 2 million homeless. The temblor lasted ten minutes, partially destroyed many villages and cities, and triggered giant waves that affected multiple countries across the Pacific Ocean.[45] The massive quake prompted the government of Chile to introduce a number of initiatives and improvements to increase the country's resilience to earthquakes, including strict seismic building codes, public education programs, and emergency preparedness practices and tools such as a tsunami warning system.[46]

In more recent years, few seismic events have proven as catastrophic and pernicious as the Indian Ocean Tsunami of 2004 and the Haiti Earthquake of 2010. Measured by how much was destroyed and the number of people killed, injured, displaced, or otherwise affected, the 2004 tsunami – with which this Element opens – was one of the most calamitous disasters triggered by a natural hazard in recent history. It is no wonder that a catastrophe of this scale would profoundly transform the urban and natural landscapes and the disaster preparedness of the Indian Ocean world. The city of Banda Aceh, the closest major urban area to the earthquake's epicenter, not only suffered the most seismic damage but also saw the greatest devastation from the force of the tsunami waves (waters reached more than 60 percent of the city at that time).[47] Much of the city's structures – constructed largely of non-engineered reinforced concrete (typical in underdeveloped or rural areas), confined masonry (common in areas of high seismic risk), and timber-framed buildings – experienced extensive structural failure or total collapse.[48] Essentially, many of those constructed to withstand seismic activity succumbed to the tsunami pressure, while those built of engineered construction that survived the tsunami nevertheless yielded to seismic forces.[49] Recovery in Banda Aceh, then – which progressed slowly at first – consisted in many ways of constructing a new city.[50] This massive reconstruction was made possible in part by the political effects of the disaster in the region. Prior to the tsunami, Aceh Province was embroiled in political conflict. From 1976 to 2005, the separatist Free Aceh Movement (Gerakan Aceh Merdeka [GAM]) fought the Indonesian

---

[44] Ibid., 26.   [45] Paul, "Valdivia Earthquake, Chile, 1960," 309–10.   [46] Ibid., 311–12.

[47] Amri and Giyarsih, "Monitoring Urban Physical Growth."

[48] Saatcioglu, Ghobarah, and Nistor, "Performance of Structures," 297.

[49] Aswathanarayana, "Overview and Integration of Part 4," 405.

[50] Umitsu, "The Tsunami Disaster," 62–3.

government for independence. After years of Indonesian military offensives that weakened the rebels, hostilities were formally brought to an end after the 2004 tsunami, which helped accelerate negotiations begun prior to the disaster.[51] This allowed authorities to focus on efforts to "build back better" (BBB)[52] and increase resilience to future hazards – efforts that, in urban areas at least,[53] have been marked by more failures than successes.[54]

Post-disaster reconstruction efforts have seen a focus on building the city back up in areas designated as safe from a potential tsunami of similar or greater scale – a worst-case scenario. For example, new spatial planning sought to establish a new main city center in the southern part of the city – away from the coast – in order to direct urban physical growth away from tsunami hazard areas, but these efforts have met significant challenges. The old city center, which lies in the hazard zone, retains to this day a high building density.[55] A long-time business district with historical buildings and landmarks, this heart of the city has proven difficult to relocate. Housing costs have also been a significant factor. Prior to the 2004 tsunami, land prices between coastal and inland areas of the city were not considerably different, but the post-disaster demand for housing in safe, inland areas in the southern parts of the city has resulted in a safe zone that is too expensive for many, and in vulnerable tsunami-affected areas that are more affordable.[56]

The result is a high level of urban growth in the hazard zones of the city and an overt transfer of disaster risk to poorer populations.[57] As of 2019, roughly 1,921 hectares (19.21 km^2) of Banda Aceh was built up in tsunami-affected zones, and 1,401 hectares (14.01 km^2) was built up in safe zones.[58] The ability of new structures to withstand the force of an earthquake or tsunami has also been called to question due to the use of inadequate building materials and a pervasive disregard for building codes and standards.[59] In the worst-affected

---

[51] Aspinall, *Islam and Nation*, 221–2.

[52] For more on this concept in post-disaster rehabilitation and reconstruction, see the UNDRR's document "Build Back Better in Recovery, Rehabilitation and Reconstruction."

[53] Local initiatives to restore mangrove forests and other coastal ecosystems to prevent deleterious effects from natural hazards such as big storms and tsunamis have been much more successful. See, for example, Pearce, "A Decade after Asian Tsunami."

[54] "It was expected that the lessons learned from the study and the recommendations based on the findings were implemented to make Aceh houses safer from future earthquakes. However, almost a decade later, recent earthquakes in Aceh have shown that these lessons were hardly incorporated in the building practices in the area, and that more serious efforts are needed to really address the safety issues of houses."

Okazaki, Pribadi, and Kusumastuti, "Safety Issues of Reconstructed Houses," 241.

[55] Amri and Giyarsih, "Monitoring Urban Physical Growth."   [56] Ibid.

[57] McCaughey, Daly, and Mundir, "Socio-economic Consequences of Post-disaster Reconstruction," 38.

[58] Amri and Giyarsih, "Monitoring Urban Physical Growth."

[59] Okazaki, Pribadi, and Kusumastuti, "Safety Issues of Reconstructed Houses," 256.

city of the 2004 tsunami then, BBB has proven more of an ideal than a reality, as urban vulnerability remains high.

However, it is not all bad news. Coastlines in Aceh Province are now less vulnerable to the effects of extreme events thanks to the planting of mangrove forests and other ecosystems that serve as natural barriers to storm surges. And throughout the Indian Ocean, affected cities and communities are now more resilient than they were before the 2004 catastrophe. Many have been rebuilt with more disaster-resistant construction and infrastructure, and new emergency alert systems across the region have helped ensure that communities are better prepared for future natural hazards. One of the factors that made the tsunami so deadly across such a large geographic space was the absence of a regional warning system that could have alerted coastal settlements throughout the Indian Ocean about the approaching waves. New early warning systems in Indonesia, Australia, India, and other nations, as well as the regional Indian Ocean Tsunami Warning System (IOTWS) launched in 2006 under the direction of international agencies and governments including the United Nations – all created in direct response to the 2004 tsunami – now provide warnings to countless communities and millions of people who in 2004 were caught completely off guard.

Just over five years later, on the other side of the planet, another powerful earthquake would trigger a massive catastrophe that similarly shocked the world, and that, more than a decade later, continues to pose countless challenges for those affected. On January 12, 2010, at 16:53, a shallow earthquake of 7.0 magnitude struck the Ouest Department of Haiti, near the town of Léogâne, roughly 30 kilometers (19 miles) from the country's capital and most populous city, Port-au-Prince. As is so often the case in the wake of disaster, the exact number of dead is unknown. Numbers range from 100,000 to 316,000 – "at least 1 out of every 30 people in the affected area" – most of them trapped in or crushed by the concrete rubble of crumbling buildings.[60] No fewer than 200,000 structures were destroyed or severely damaged, displacing approximately 1.8 million people.[61]

It was a cataclysmic disaster that left an indelible mark on the nation's psyche. Among the people of Haiti, the earthquake goes by many names. Some refer to it as *12 janvye* (January 12) or simply the *tranbleman de tè* (earthquake).[62] Others avoid naming it altogether and speak of it only as *goudougoudou* (a reference to the sound of the rumbling earth), or *bagay la*, literally, "the thing."[63] Whatever people call it, the disaster was not merely the

---

[60] Payton, "Concrete Kleptocracy and Haiti's Culture of Building," 71.
[61] Versluis, "Haiti Earthquake, 2010," 137.
[62] Kinsley Jean, personal communication, February 6, 2022.
[63] Trouillot, "Eternity Lasted Less Than Sixty Seconds," 312.

result of the shaking of the earth but of historical processes dating, in this case, to the late fifteenth-century arrival of Europeans on the island, and especially to the seventeenth-century founding by the French of the colony of Saint-Domingue (which became the Republic of Haiti after the Haitian Revolution).[64] Since then, a history of colonialism, slavery, exploitation, foreign intervention, corruption, poverty, and inequality have produced a country that is uniquely vulnerable to its natural hazards – which is why anthropologist and disaster studies expert Anthony Oliver-Smith has called the 2010 tremor "Haiti's 500-Year Earthquake."[65]

On *12 janvye*, Haiti was completely unprepared for a hazard of this scale. The nation – the poorest in the Western Hemisphere – had no building codes in place to protect its structures and its people from seismic hazards, and standards for building and materials were difficult to enforce.[66] There was also no documented understanding of the nation's vulnerability to earthquakes. Prior to 2010, it had been at least 150 years since the greater Port-au-Prince area experienced a temblor of similar magnitude,[67] yet, since 1950 alone, the region has seen no fewer than eighteen major storms.[68] Aside from the occasional small tremor then, no recent collective memory existed of a seismic disaster that could have spurred efforts to reinforce the Republic's built environment. Instead, dangerous weather seemed a much more immediate threat. Accordingly, most of the structures destroyed in the densely populated, worst-affected cities of Léogâne and Port-au-Prince were constructed of unreinforced masonry or poor-quality concrete blocks – rigid edifices that proved deadly during the tremor.[69]

In fact, the homes of Haiti's poorest, often made of reclaimed materials or mud walls with thatched roofs, proved safer for their occupants (if not more resilient) than those of the country's middle- and upper-income groups who

---

[64] Oliver-Smith, "Haiti's 500-Year Earthquake," 18–23; Payton, "Concrete Kleptocracy and Haiti's Culture of Building," 72.

> [T]he true causes of Haiti's poverty and instability are not mysterious, and they have nothing to do with any inherent shortcomings on the part of the Haitians themselves. Rather, Haiti's present is the product of its history: of the nation's founding by enslaved people who overthrew their masters and freed themselves; of the hostility that this revolution generated among the colonial powers surrounding the country; and of the intense struggle within Haiti itself to define that freedom and realize its promise. Dubois, *Haiti*, 4.

[65] Oliver-Smith, "Haiti's 500-Year Earthquake," 18–23; Payton, "Concrete Kleptocracy and Haiti's Culture of Building," 72.

[66] Payton, "Concrete Kleptocracy and Haiti's Culture of Building," 78.

[67] Versluis, "Haiti Earthquake, 2010," 138.

[68] Payton, "Concrete Kleptocracy and Haiti's Culture of Building," 76.

[69] Following the earthquake, scientists and engineers pointed to the poor quality of Haiti's concrete as a contributing factor to the earthquake's devastation. Ibid., 77.

occupied the concrete structures.[70] This was especially true for residents of Haiti's more sparsely populated areas, who had easier access to safer, open spaces than those in more densely inhabited areas lined with narrow streets and alleyways.[71] The country's vulnerability was further aggravated by its inadequate medical and search-and-rescue infrastructures.

Today, Haiti is at risk of repeating this history. Its population remains largely urban, poor, and underserved. Building standards are difficult to carry out and enforce, and thousands still live in displaced persons' camps. Meanwhile, international aid has proven inadequate at best, a dismal failure at worst, plagued by disorder and corruption.

In Haiti as elsewhere, the most immediate danger of earthquake and tsunami hazards to human settlements – whether urban or rural – is the destruction of built environments. Residential structures in particular are nearly always destroyed in the greatest numbers. Most earthquake casualties thus result from the collapse of buildings, and, among the most seriously affected survivors, those who are left homeless represent the majority.[72] The latter is also true of tsunami survivors, although the most common cause of death in these instances is drowning and the cause of most injuries is contact with debris.

Damage during an earthquake or tsunami (or indeed any of a number of other hazards, including hurricanes, floods, etc.) may be further aggravated by the destruction of roads, fuel lines, power lines, communication systems, and water and wastewater systems, as well as hospitals, schools, retail stores, and numerous other public service buildings and critical infrastructures. In urban areas, home to more resources and extensive networks of critical infrastructures that serve exponentially more people than in rural areas, the damage and suffering from the destruction or disruption of these "built life-lines" are only multiplied.[73] And because vulnerability is not equally distributed, when disaster strikes, it is the poor, along with women, children, and racial, ethnic, and religious minorities who suffer most and are most likely to be displaced.

Whether resulting from an earthquake or any other major hazard, disasters change cities. At times, it is true, destroyed communities may be reconstructed in the same location, and/or in the same manner or of the same materials that led to its crumbling in the first place. Yet at other times, they are reerected in new, safer locations and are constructed to be more resistant to the effects of a hazard. When lessons are learned following a major catastrophe, and when these lessons go as far as influencing urban policy, planning, and development – and there is never any guarantee that they will – cities can emerge more resilient

---

[70] Ibid., 83.   [71] Versluis, "Haiti Earthquake, 2010," 138–9.
[72] Hewitt, *Regions of Risk*, 202.   [73] Ibid., 204.

than they were previously. New zoning laws, building codes, and other regulations or practices, in turn, can change the layout, the appearance, and even the character of a city – if too often at the expense of minority and low-SES communities. With promises of recovery, renewal, and improvement, disaster opportunists – be they politicians, investors, corporations, developers and so forth – do not always proceed with everyone's best interest in mind.[74]

Major catastrophes can also lead to the migration of significant portions of the population, a phenomenon that can alter the culture, demographics, and economy of urban areas – not only the point of departure but the destination – in enduring ways. This occurred in the aftermath of Hurricane Katrina, when as many as 250,000 people fled the city. Of the roughly 175,000 of these who were African American, at least 75,000 never returned. This great migration has had profound long-term effects on the city of New Orleans, resulting, for example, in a dwindling Black middle class and in a city that is smaller and more white than it was prior to 2005.[75] Section 3 continues our discussion on urban disasters by looking at some of the ways in which cities around the world have experienced and been changed by catastrophes related to wind and water, especially floods and tropical cyclones.[76]

3 Wind and Water

Beginning in July 1931, one of the worst flood disasters in history unfolded over central and eastern China. The 1931 China floods, or the Yangzi–Huai Flood Disaster (as it is most commonly known in China), was a national catastrophe that ultimately affected waterways throughout the country. A series of strong storms in the summer combined with heavy snowmelt from the western highlands and an unusually wet spring to further augment an already engorged

---

[74] A number of important texts have explored this unsettling issue. See, for example, Klein, *The Shock Doctrine*; Horowitz, *Katrina*; Rozario, *Culture of Calamity*; Steinberg, *Acts of God*; essays in Remes and Horowitz, *Critical Disaster Studies*; Loewenstein, *Disaster Capitalism*. While not dealing directly with the subject of disasters, Naomi Oreskes and Erik Conway's monumental study on campaigns to sow doubt among the public and to obfuscate truths about various issues to suit corporate interests and political agendas is as important and as it is revealing. See Oreskes and Conway, *Merchants of Doubt*.

[75] Casselman, "Katrina Washed Away New Orleans's Black Middle Class."

[76] The term "tropical cyclone" describes any "rotating, organized system of clouds and thunderstorms that originates over tropical or subtropical waters and has closed, low-level circulation." The terms "hurricane" and "typhoon" thus refer to the same weather phenomenon: a tropical cyclone. The only difference is where it occurs. If the cyclone develops in the North Atlantic, central North Pacific, or eastern North Pacific, we call it a hurricane. If it develops in the Northwest Pacific, it is called a typhoon. And if it develops in the South Pacific or Indian Ocean, we refer to it as a tropical cyclone. National Ocean Service, National Oceanic and Atmospheric Administration (NOAA), "What Is the Difference between a Hurricane and a Typhoon?" https://oceanservice.noaa.gov/facts/cyclone.html.

Yangzi (Yangtze) River.[77] Occurring in one of the most populous regions in the world, and affecting an area of approximately 180,000 square kilometers (69,498 square miles) – equivalent to the size of England and half of Scotland, or the combined America states of New York, New Jersey, and Connecticut – the massive floods soon resulted in a cascade of subsequent disasters, including fires, famine, and epidemics.[78] Over a series of months, the deluge affected as many as 53 million people and took the lives of roughly 2 million. Hundreds of thousands drowned while others died of blunt trauma. Yet it was the disaster's secondary consequences – most notably, starvation and disease – that claimed the most lives. In some areas, illnesses such as cholera, measles, and malaria alone were responsible for as much as 70 percent of deaths.[79]

The city of Wuhan, the capital of Hubei Province in central China, was one of the worst affected. Here, in inland China's most technologically advanced city, the "Chicago of the East," floodwaters, hunger, pests, and disease combined with a series of additional risks unique to the urban landscape – such as chemical fires and collapsing pylons and wires – to create an exceptionally perilous situation.[80] When the dykes that encircled Wuhan collapsed in late July, the water that had been held back suddenly gushed in, submerging much of the city and turning its streets into canals that for months were overrun with small boats called sampans.[81] Local police tried to direct traffic and maintain order in the city's new aqueous thoroughfares. Initially, they stood on boxes, then, as floodwaters grew, they climbed onto tree branches. Soon, however, the water reached such depths that authorities could do little as boats collected in the city center. One of these sailed into the Texaco oil depository and started a fire that burned on the water for three days.[82]

To add to the misery, floodwaters soon combined with the city's sewage, creating a catastrophic public health crisis. In addition, much of the local railway line was destroyed, the city's electrical system failed, and its telegraph office, telephone exchange, and airport were forced to close. Wuhan was thus left with no electricity and no access to communication or travel. Amid this watery hellscape, the city was awash in its vulnerability.

Inadequate building standards, not only in Wuhan but across the flood zone, rendered many structures susceptible to the torrent of water.[83] The most

---

[77] "As much rain fell in one month as would normally be expected in one and a half years." Courtney, *The Nature of Disaster in China*, 5.

[78] Ibid., 3.

[79] Ibid., 4–5, 250. The exact number of dead will never be known, but historian Chris Courtney has noted that the more commonly cited numbers range from 140,000 to 4 million.

[80] Ibid., 11.   [81] Courtney, "Picturing Disaster."   [82] Ibid.

[83] Courtney, *The Nature of Disaster in China*, 51, 61.

vulnerable were low-standing small huts or earthen homes that not only proved weak against the flood waves but were also most likely to be situated on the most flood-prone and therefore the most affordable land[84] – a recurring pattern in the history of disasters, as the most hazard-prone, potentially dangerous areas are often also home to society's poorest and most vulnerable. Meanwhile, the homes of the region's wealthier residents – including taller homes and multi-story buildings – not only proved more (if not entirely) resilient against the floodwaters but could also serve as safe havens for those who could make their way to the roofs.[85]

City officials soon devised both short-term and long-term solutions to help manage the catastrophe and to prevent it from happening again. While the waters still raged, the city's business community played an integral role in the raising of funds and the organization of flood relief. Their most notable short-term achievement was the construction of wooden walkways that would allow city residents to walk over the flooded streets (Figure 2).[86] In the longer term, authorities set themselves to the construction of more effective dams, levees, and other flood-protection structures. Following the disaster, for example, tens of thousands of workers and soldiers were deployed to reinforce Wuhan's dykes.[87] In subsequent decades, reed huts and earthen homes were increasingly replaced with more resilient structures; human- or ox-powered pumps were exchanged for motorized and electrical water pumps that allowed farmers to drain the land more efficiently; and increased government oversight led to the regularization and standardization of the hydraulic network.[88] As evidenced by the 2008 Sichuan earthquake that resulted in the deaths of more than 80,000 people, all too many vulnerabilities remain in China as a result of underfunding, corruption, discrimination, or gross negligence. Yet by the end of the century, the aforementioned developments and others had helped reduce flood mortality rates from the millions to the thousands – a feat that is simultaneously impressive and grossly inadequate.[89]

In questions of vulnerability, not all cities are created equal. While any urban landscape will prove more impervious than the natural land surface, where hazards of wind and water are concerned, cities that are particularly low-lying in relation to sea level or that are situated along a coast or near a major waterway or dam are especially susceptible. Among these, few are more exposed than the city of New Orleans. Located on the Gulf Coast of the United States, positioned along the Mississippi River, encircled by a network of levees and floodwalls,

---

[84] Ibid., 4, 61–2.   [85] Ibid., 61–2.   [86] Courtney, "Picturing Disaster."
[87] Courtney, *The Nature of Disaster in China*, 237.   [88] Ibid., 241.
[89] Ibid., 245, 246. Special thanks to Chris Courtney for reading a draft of this section.

Figure 2 Image depicting a walkway constructed over the floodwaters and the sampans (boats) used to navigate the streets-turned-canals. As shown in Courtney, "Picturing Disaster: The 1931 Wuhan Flood," *China Dialogue*, https://chinadialogue.net/en/cities/10811-picturing-disaster-the-1931-wuhan-flood. Used with permission from the author.

and sitting partially below sea level, the Crescent City is no stranger to the risks that derive from both its natural and its built environment.

Throughout its long and eventful disaster history, New Orleans has experienced more than its fair share of major floods, epidemics, tornadoes, heat waves, oil spills, and fires (one of which I discuss in Section 4), but its exposure to cyclones is perhaps its foremost weakness. Across the Gulf Coast and the Caribbean basin, each hurricane season (June through November) brings trepidation. Already by the spring, local news outlets, utility company emails, and even supermarket leaflets begin issuing their annual reminders to prepare. But as a tropical storm grows into a major hurricane and a hurricane watch becomes a hurricane warning, there is only so much most people can do to ready their homes and themselves for what comes next.

When Hurricane Katrina made landfall in Louisiana on August 29, 2005, most New Orleanians could not have prepared for the catastrophe that would soon befall them. Although sustained winds may not have exceeded 129 kilometers (80 miles) per hour, by the time the eye of the hurricane arrived 32 kilometers (20 miles) outside of New Orleans, the city's levee system could not sustain the force of the storm.[90] When it collapsed, the city was inundated. Hundreds were killed, tens of thousands of homes were destroyed, and the entire spectacle played out on people's television sets, unfolding like a Greek tragedy rife with misery, adversity, and political allegory.

The heart-wrenching scenes of bloated bodies floating in the floodwaters were not entirely for naught. Hurricane Katrina did more to alert the average person in the United States about the role of humans in disaster-making than perhaps any previous disaster. For many who followed the drama, the racism, political ineptitude, and sheer negligence that were most fundamentally responsible for the calamity were on full display. This is one of the reasons "Katrina" has earned such a prominent place in disaster literature.[91] The catastrophe has offered important lessons about the complexity of environmental racism.

In his book *Dumping in Dixie*, sociologist Robert D. Bullard defines environmental racism as "any policy, practice or directive that differentially affects or disadvantages (whether intended or unintended) individuals, groups, or communities based on race or color."[92] Sometimes, the links are not quite so apparent, however. When the levees broke, it was not only Black and poor communities that were flooded but also those of white suburban and middle-class people. In fact, the city's public housing, situated in older parts of the city and home to New Orleans' poorest, were largely spared the worst of the flooding.[93] In *Katrina: A History, 1915–2015*, Andy Horowitz explains it best:

> The flood was not the result of racist policies or practices in the years directly before the levee breaches in 2005. Rather, racism in federal housing policies from the 1930s through the 1960s – including redlining, segregation, and Veterans Affairs loans that went disproportionately to white people – all enabled the white middle class to move into new homes. Since the only available land was on lower ground in new neighborhoods and suburbs, these homes were located there, while many African Americans continued to live in the [less-desirable, older] inner city [that sat] on higher ground.[94]

Katrina – with its long history and enduring legacy – is a lesson in the revealing nature of disasters, particularly as regards the role of humans in the construction of risk, vulnerability, and, therefore, catastrophe.

The storm triggered or accelerated a number of important changes in New Orleans. Among these, public housing apartment buildings were demolished,

---

[90] Horowitz, *Katrina*, 118.
[91] Countless important studies from across disciplines have sought to make sense of the tragedy. In his 2020 book on the subject, historian Andy Horowitz traces the history of Hurricane Katrina to a century earlier and demonstrates how very far from inevitable the catastrophe was.
[92] Bullard, *Dumping in Dixie*, 98.   [93] Horowitz, *Katrina*, 7.   [94] Ibid.

leaving hundreds displaced; 4,300 teachers along with hundreds of staffers were fired as the city's public school system was replaced with a network of independently run public charter schools; the Army Corps of Engineers constructed a new levee system "while the wetlands beyond the walls continued to erode and the city itself continued to sink."[95] Significant changes also came in the form of demographic shifts. As mentioned earlier, the aftermath of the storm saw an exodus of hurricane survivors that has changed the demographic makeup of the city. According to the US Census, the African American population fell by 36.5 percent between 2000 and 2010, while the white population fell by 16.6 percent. In the 2010 census, African Americans represented 60.2 percent of the population, down from 67.3 percent in 2000.[96] And between 2010 and 2020, the white, non-Latinx population of Orleans Parish – coterminous with the city of New Orleans proper – grew by 15.9 percent, while the African American population grew by only 0.5 percent.[97] White residents now make up a larger proportion of the population than they did before the storm, "which [has] literally changed the color of the electoral politics in the city."[98] Meanwhile, the Latinx population grew by 3,225 between the 2000 and 2010 censuses, made up largely of those who arrived seeking work after the storm and decided to stay.[99] The damage was so extensive that the federal government suspended various labor regulations to accelerate recovery.[100] From there, the number has only grown, with the Latinx-identifying population rising by 12,966 in Orleans Parish between 2010 and 2020 (and a whopping 54,761 across the New Orleans metropolitan area).[101] In terms of population, the city is now smaller, less Black (though still predominantly so), and more white and Latino than it was before Katrina.

A similar exodus ensued in 2017 after Hurricane Maria devastated the island of Puerto Rico, destroying its power grid and plunging much of the population into darkness for months. Just two weeks after Hurricane Irma left a trail of destruction across parts of the Caribbean, Hurricane Maria spun through the region as a Category 5 storm, causing catastrophic damage and nearly wiping out the island of Dominica. From there, the cyclone moved toward Puerto Rico, where it made landfall on September 20, 2017, near Yabucoa in the southeastern

---

[95] Horowitz, *Katrina*, 4.   [96] Ibid., 169, 174.

[97] Plyer, "Population Shifts across Metro New Orleans."   [98] Cobb, "Race and the Storm."

[99] Plyer, "What Census 2010 Reveals," 2.

[100] Nowakowski, "Charts Show How Hurricane Katrina Changed New Orleans."

[101] Plyer, "Population Shifts across Metro New Orleans." The departure of New Orleanians in the wake of Hurricane Katrina has also changed the cities to which they relocated. Among these, Houston stands out for having taken in the greatest numbers. The impact of Katrina survivors on the city attracted media attention in the years that followed. See, for example, Hamilton, "The Huddled Masses"; Patterson, "Katrina Evacuees Shift Houston's Identity."

part of the island, as a Category 4 storm with wind speeds of up to 249.4 kilometers per hour (155 miles per hour).

The capital city, San Juan, saw widespread flooding – waist high in some parts – as well as downed trees, traffic lights, and electricity poles that obstructed roads and highways. Windows and glass doors across the city were shattered and even the concrete walls of some condominiums blew off, leaving former living spaces exposed.[102] Throughout the island, homes, schools, businesses, and hospitals were destroyed, and extensive damage to electricity and communication infrastructures – including cellular service and the Internet – left Puerto Ricans disconnected and in the dark.[103] With no power, potable water, communication, or health services to speak of, the island descended into a major humanitarian crisis that was only compounded by a stunted and disorganized federal response.[104] Although the reported number of deaths tied directly to the disaster sat at 64 for months after the storm, this number was officially changed to 2,975 after an excess mortality study conducted by researchers at George Washington University and the University of Puerto Rico in 2018 determined that the number was in fact much higher.[105]

Hurricanes Irma and Maria led to a "historic net migration loss" as island residents departed for the mainland of the United States in record numbers.[106] Estimates vary, but in the first year alone, roughly 160,000 people left, which represents more than twice the number of permanent relocations in the previous two years.[107] The Pew Research Center estimates that the population of Puerto Rico declined by 3.9 percent in 2018 – the largest annual drop since 1950, when the data began to be collected. Moreover, the island's 2018 population of 3.2 million represents its lowest point since 1979.[108] The rapid depopulation

---

[102] Ferré-Sadurní and Hartocollis, "Maria Strikes, and Puerto Rico Goes Dark."

[103] Hinojosa, "Two Sides of the Coin of Puerto Rican Migration," 236; Acosta et al., "Quantifying the Dynamics," 32775.

[104] The incompetence and inefficiency of the federal response stands in contrast to the administration's own claims about its perceived successes. See, for example, Graham, "Trump's Dubious Revisionist History." For a timeline of the federal response in the first two weeks after landfall, see Meyer, "What's Happening with the Relief Effort in Puerto Rico?" San Juan mayor Carmen Yulín Cruz was among the island's most outspoken critics of the administration's slow response. See, for example, Hernández, Berman, and Wagner, "San Juan Mayor Slams Trump Administration"; Hoyos, "100 days after Hurricane Maria"; Vazquez, "San Juan Mayor."

[105] Milken Institute School of Public Health, "Ascertainment of the Estimated Excess Mortality," iii, 9.

[106] Flores and Krogstad, "Puerto Rico's Population Declined Sharply after Hurricanes Maria and Irma."

[107] Hinojosa and Meléndez, "Puerto Rican Exodus," 1. Within the island too, the storms accelerated a general shift in population from rural to urban areas, in part because infrastructural damage was greater in the countryside. Acosta et al., "Quantifying the Dynamics of Migration," 32774.

[108] Flores and Krogstad, "Puerto Rico's Population Declined Sharply after Hurricanes Maria and Irma."

has only aggravated the island's preexisting economic woes and accelerated the disappearance of government services and employment, as well as the closing of schools and businesses.[109] Such developments in turn have augmented unemployment and poverty on the island, causing even more residents to leave. It is a vicious cycle.

Such great movements of people change not only the regions they leave behind but also their destinations. In the storm's aftermath, Puerto Ricans relocated to cities across the mainland. According to the 2017 US Census Bureau's American Community Survey (ACS), the majority relocated to Florida (30 percent), followed by Pennsylvania (10 percent), Massachusetts (7 percent), Texas (7 percent), Connecticut (6 percent), New York (6 percent), New Jersey (5 percent), Ohio (3 percent), Maryland (3 percent), and Georgia (3 percent).[110] A different data set based on mobile phone use found that those who first moved to Florida represented 43 percent, followed by 9 percent for New York, 7 percent for Texas, and 6 percent for Pennsylvania, but these numbers include those who eventually returned to Puerto Rico.[111] Nevertheless, a few cities stand out for having received the most migrants. Within Florida, the greatest numbers arrived in Orlando (22 percent), followed by Osceola County, especially the city of Kissimmee (15 percent), and Miami (10 percent). Of those who went to New York State, 66 percent chose New York City, "with the Bronx being the leading destination" among the five boroughs or counties.[112]

In Central Florida – already a center of Puerto Rican culture in the mainland United States – the sudden influx placed significant pressure on housing, social services, schools, traffic, and the job market, which have in turn helped shape developments in the region in recent years.[113] The rapid growth in population led to calls for more housing, bilingual teachers, health and social services and professionals, among other resources, and has reinforced Greater Orlando's (Orlando-Kissimmee-Sanford Metropolitan Statistical Area) position as one of the fastest-growing metropolitan areas in the United States. According to Orlando Economic Partnership, from 2018 to 2019, Greater Orlando grew by 2.4 percent – four times the rate of growth of the United States.[114] Puerto Ricans have also helped to shape the region politically, as these American citizens tend to lean Democratic. The full impact of Hurricane Maria, like that of Katrina, the

---

[109] Hinojosa and Meléndez, "Puerto Rican Exodus," 6–7.

[110] Hinojosa, "Two Sides of the Coin of Puerto Rican Migration," 246–7.

[111] Echenique and Melgar, "Mapping Puerto Rico's Hurricane Migration with Mobile Phone Data."

[112] Ibid.

[113] Sisson, "Puerto Rican Exodus to Central Florida Begs Question"; Alvarez, "A Great Migration from Puerto Rico."

[114] Fleming, "Why Orlando's Growth Rate Is the Second Fastest of the 30 Largest U.S. Cities."

Haiti Earthquake, or any other major disaster, is thus ongoing, and the full extent of its implications remains to be seen.[115]

To truly understand a disaster's ramifications, then, and relationships between catastrophe and the city, it is not enough to look at ground zero or to focus on the short term. A disaster's effects can spread like seismic waves, covering much more geographic space and causing much longer-term implications, than at first it may appear. In order to more fully appreciate the true impact of an extreme event, it is necessary to trace these waves across time and space, looking outward at the larger picture. Shifting to the topic of urban conflagrations, Section 4 looks at urban vulnerability to fire and explores some of the ways in which fires and their threat have helped shape our cities in the long term.

4 Urban Infernos

Environmental historian and fire expert Stephen Pyne once wrote:

> The built landscape is as much a fire environment as forests and fields. It can hardly be otherwise: the hearth, the house, the town – all are designed with fire in mind. Most seek to promote contained fire but, if anything, are more fire-prone than the countryside around them. After all, crowding people together boosts the density of open fires, and cramming structures packs more fuels ever closer. In brief, cities are and have always been fire places.[116]

Humans have been building "with fire in mind" for thousands of years – centering their homes around a hearth that allows for cooking, keeping warm, heating water, and illuminating the night – yet fire disasters remain a considerable threat, due in part to planning, design, and construction practices that do not take fire hazards sufficiently into account. And the threat is only getting worse as humans move into more fire-prone regions and as climate change increases the occurrence and intensity of wildfires that reach towns and cities.

In the long history of urban fires, many cities stand out for the extent to which they emerged transformed from the ashes. One example that has received relatively little attention took place in New Orleans during its time as a colonial port city of Spain.[117] Although the French laid the colonial city's foundations, it was the Spanish who most dramatically built upon it into the beginning of the nineteenth century. The fire took place on March 21, 1788, a blustery Good Friday, as groups of people congregated in and around the Saint Louis parish church and the Plaza de Armas, or Place D'Armes as many still

---

[115] For a valuable study on the experiences of Puerto Ricans in the first months after Hurricane Maria, based on firsthand accounts, see Valle, "¡Puerto Rico Se Levanta!"

[116] Pyne, *Fire*, 102.

[117] For more on this disaster, see Ermus, "Spanish Foundations of the French Quarter," from which parts of this section are excerpted.

called it (today's Jackson Square).[118] It began in the home of Spanish royal treasurer Don Vicente Jose Nuñez, on 619 Chartres Street, where around 1:30 in the afternoon, his burning wax tapers either reached the drapes that hung nearby or ignited the ceiling. "[From here] proceeded the destruction of the most regular, well-governed small city in the Western world," as one eyewitness described it.[119] Across town, residents rushed to salvage as much property as possible, but in eighteenth-century New Orleans, it was their enslaved people who largely carried out the operation. In the end, the calamitous episode took few lives but devastated 856 of about 1,100 buildings. Much of the population was left homeless, and the Spanish government was left with the major task of aiding the victims, rebuilding the city, and funding the entire enterprise.

In eighteenth-century New Orleans, as in other colonial towns, the fire was an accident waiting to happen. Little care had been taken in the city's history to protect it against conflagration. Despite the fact that the colonial capital was constructed mostly of wood, few efforts were made to enact safety measures that would prevent a major fire. Throughout the late 1770s and 1780s, Spanish colonial officials proposed safer building codes and the purchase and safekeeping of leather buckets and ladders, but the proposals were mostly sidelined.[120] On the eve of the fire, extinguishing equipment was either scarce or nonexistent. According to contemporary accounts, almost no buckets were found during the several hours of frantic panic that took hold of the city, and not a single fire engine was in place to assist in the massive undertaking of extinguishing the uncontrollable flames that raged into the evening – the two that existed were consumed by the flames before they could be secured.

In the British North American colonies, cities including Boston, Philadelphia, and New York experienced fires in the sixteenth to eighteenth centuries, and all implemented policies to prevent and combat fires as a result. Settled much earlier than New Orleans, these towns were much more experienced with the reality of urban fires, and by the beginning of the eighteenth century, they had already formed private fire clubs and kept several fire engines

---

[118] The first church to stand at this site was erected by the French in 1718, two years before it was established as a parish. Construction for the larger church, completed in the *colombage sur sole* style, began in 1725 and was completed in 1727. This is the church that was destroyed in the fire of 1788.

[119] "Extract of a Letter from New Orleans Dated March 26," *The London Chronicle*, August 19–21, 1788, Williams Research Center (hereafter cited as WRC), Colonial Louisiana Newspaper Collection.

[120] For these records, see New Orleans Public Library, City Archives, hereafter cited as NOPL, *Alphabetical and Chronological Digest of the Acts & Deliberations of the Cabildo, 1769–1803*, book 1: passim; book 2: 52, 60; book 3: passim.

(eleven in New York and ten in Boston) on hand in case of disaster.[121] In 1788, however, New Orleans had yet to experience its own major fire.

It took the conflagration of 1788 for the Spanish government in New Orleans to implement new fire safety tools, policies, and practices. These included fire buckets and fire engines that would be supervised by *Alcaldes de Carrio* or commissaries of police.[122] New Orleans also saw a new patrol system of night watchmen or *serenos*, whose responsibility it was to preserve the peace, keep the streetlamps burning on moonless nights, and sound the general alarm in case of fire.[123] On the eve of the fire, New Orleans was largely constructed of wood or *colombage*, which, on Good Friday 1788, served only as fuel for the flames that destroyed the capital. As a result, in the months and years that followed the devastation, efforts were made to establish building regulations that restricted the use of wood and encouraged that of brick or of cement-covered timber frames with brick filling between posts.

After a second large fire in 1794 that destroyed various large buildings, new regulations requiring that all structures be constructed of brick were better enforced, and only roofs of tile or other fireproof materials were permitted.[124] In this way, the Spanish turned New Orleans into "a neighborhood of brick buildings."[125] The 1788 fire also led to a major rethinking of the city. Because Spanish administration directed reconstruction efforts after the fire, the city took on new architecturally Spanish characteristics. These include the pastel-colored exteriors, arched entryways, Andaluz-style inner courtyards and open patios that served as external rooms and passageways, and the intricate, lacy iron grillwork balconies so characteristic of New Orleans today.[126]

The typical Spanish styles that emerged in the city after the fire are found elsewhere in the Atlantic world, particularly across Central and South America and parts of the Caribbean. Cities that share New Orleans' architectural characteristics include Havana, Cuba; Quito, Ecuador; Ciudad Colonial in Santo Domingo (Dominican Republic); Cartagena, Colombia; Casco Antiguo in Panama City; Old San Juan, Puerto Rico, and a great many others. Even in Louisiana, Spanish architectural influence extended beyond the Vieux Carré (Old Square [another name for the French Quarter]). As late as the mid-nineteenth century, "the Spanish-plan Creole plantation house was still the most popular type of 'big house' built in wealthy and conservative St. Charles Parish."[127]

---

[121] Carp, "Fire of Liberty," 782.

[122] NOPL, *Digest of the Acts*, April 18, 1788, book 3, vol. II, 21.

[123] Kerr, *Petty Felony, Slave Defiance, and Frontier Villainy*, 178.

[124] NOPL, *Digest of the Acts*, October 2, 1795, book 4, vol. I, 53–5. Several deliberations discuss the implementation of new building codes and the problems of enforcing them. On roofing regulations, see ibid., July 29, 1796, book 4, vol. I, 141.

[125] Toledano, *A Pattern Book of New Orleans Architecture*, 159.   [126] Ibid.

[127] Edwards, "The Origins of Creole Architecture," 9.

Since the eighteenth century, however, several other architectural characteristics have contributed to the city's appearance, including Creole, French, and American townhouse styles, thereby giving it a unique flavor. Some of the architectural elements in New Orleans that are less uniquely Spanish include side gables and the steeply pitched, non-tiled and mansard roofs installed later in the city's history. Nevertheless, it was in the later Spanish period, after the Good Friday Fire, that New Orleans began to see the appearance of the typically narrow, three-story brick buildings referred to as Creole townhouses, set at property lines, that replaced the previous freestanding structures of the French period.[128] Many of New Orleans' most prominent and recognizable buildings, such as the Presbytère and the Spanish Cabildo (today's Louisiana State Museum), were erected over the ashes of earlier French ones under Spanish administration and with Spanish funding. While most structures in the Vieux Carré today are not the same ones erected in the colonial period, construction in the quarter has since succeeded at maintaining the integrity of the city's inherited Spanish colonial styles, even as these have been combined with newer architectural influences.

Before March 21, 1788, the colonial capital was already undergoing a series of structural and cultural transformations. After the conflagration, however, these changes accelerated. The city not only began to take on the aesthetic that we recognize today, but also began to expand in terms of size, population, and commercial relations faster than ever before. The Good Friday Fire was thus a major, transformative event that helped create the modern port city of New Orleans.[129]

In the following century, a larger, much more famous fire would transform another North American city in enduring ways. On October 8, 1871, on a windy Sunday evening amid a long period of drought, firefighters responded to an alarm at Patrick and Catherine O'Leary's cow barn on the southwest side of Chicago. The fire, fueled by the city's parched timber and southeasterly winds, spread quickly and uncontrollably until it devastated more than 9 square kilometers (3 square miles) of the city, including its downtown.[130] In about thirty hours, it destroyed more than 18,000 buildings, left roughly 100,000 (out of 300,000) people homeless, and took nearly 300 lives.[131] Then as now, the precise cause of the fire was unknown, though plenty of unfounded speculation ensued, much of it revealing ethnic, class, gendered, racial, and religious tensions in the city.[132]

---

[128] For more on Spanish Creole architecture, see ibid. Also see Toledano, *A Pattern Book of New Orleans Architecture*. On New Orleans architecture in general, see Wilson, *The Vieux Carré*.

[129] Ermus, "Spanish Foundations of the French Quarter."

[130] Sawislak, *Smoldering City*, 2, 29.   [131] Ibid., 2.

[132] For more on this, see, for example, Sawislak, *Smoldering City*; Smith, *Chicago's Great Fire*.

Figure 3 R. P. Studley Co. "Map showing the burnt district in Chicago: published for the benefit of the Relief Fund," oriented with north to the right (Saint Louis: R. P. Studley, 187–?). Map. Library of Congress. www.loc.gov /item/2010592712

In this way, urban fires are unique. Whereas other types of disasters – earthquakes, storms, droughts, wildfires, or volcanic eruptions – are more likely to be perceived as naturally occurring or as acts of God, it is more often human activity that gets the blame for causing fires in the city.[133] In the aftermath of the Peshtigo Fire, for example – a forest fire that began on the same day but affected a much smaller and more homogenous logging town in Wisconsin – few if any scapegoats were sought despite its taking many more lives (approximately 1,500) and scorching well over a million acres.[134] In Chicago, it was humans and human activity that were largely inculpated.

On the eve of the fire, Chicago was almost entirely combustible. Its urban landscape was built primarily of wood, which served to fuel the flames that would raze the city to the ground (Figure 4). The exception was its downtown, which was constructed largely of stone and brick – nonflammable materials that are normally better suited to withstand a blaze – yet this fire-resistant district

---

[133] Sawislak, *Smoldering City*, 43. It is worth noting that there are always exceptions. During the Black Death in fourteenth-century Europe, anti-Semitic pogroms in some towns were fueled by false rumors that Jews were poisoning the local wells. And in times of disaster more broadly, whether it be earthquakes, plagues, or floods, there have always been those who blame local sinners (prostitutes, drunkards, etc.) and others for their misfortune.

[134] Sawislak, *Smoldering City*, 43; Pyne, *Fire in America*, 206.

Figure 4 The Chicago Fire, 1871, plate no. 3. Gelatin silver print. Library of
Congress. http://loc.gov/pictures/resource/cph.3a40635

would not be spared from the devastation.[135] Some hours after it began, the
Chicago fire became so large and intense that it developed into a firestorm –
a phenomenon so hot and powerful that it crumbled marble, melted iron, and
dissolved the mortar of brick buildings, collapsing structures throughout the city
center.[136] One survivor later related that "the very air was full of flame."[137]
Another recounted, "The air was like that of a furnace – fearfully hot."[138]

On October 11, three days after the fire began, the *Chicago Tribune* ran its
first postfire editorial. Titled simply "CHEER UP," it promised in capital letters
that "CHICAGO SHALL RISE AGAIN" (Figure 5):

> Already contracts have been made for rebuilding some of the burned blocks, and
> the clearing away of the debris will begin to-day ... The money and securities in
> all the banks are safe. The railroads are working with all their energies to bring us
> out of our affliction. The three hundred millions of capital invested in these roads
> is bound to see us through ... CHICAGO MUST RISE AGAIN.[139]

---

[135] Sawislak, *Smoldering City*, 1.
[136] Ibid., 26–7. As we saw in Section 1, a similar firestorm occurred in Lisbon in the aftermath of
the 1755 earthquake.
[137] As quoted in ibid., 26.   [138] Smith, *Chicago's Great Fire*, 82.
[139] "CHEER UP," *Chicago Tribune*, October 11, 1871.

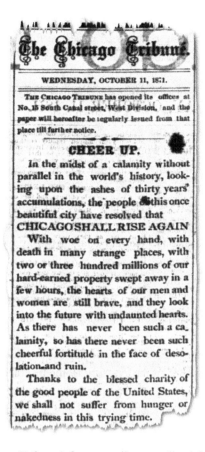

Figure 5 The *Chicago Tribune's* first post-disaster editorial aimed for optimism
amid the devastation. It concluded, "The worst is already over. In a few days
more all the dangers will be past, and we can resume the battle of life with
Christian faith and Western grit. Let us all cheer up!" "CHEER UP," *Chicago
Tribune*, October 11, 1871. As pictured in www.chicagotribune.com/news/ct-
great-chicago-fire-cheer-up-editorial-20210820-f2emncydkzg45arl4x
x6ektrpe-story.html

Indeed, Chicago did rise again – and in dramatic fashion – but contrary to popular
understandings of the fire as immediately giving way to a state-of-the-art city of
skyscrapers, significant changes did not occur overnight. It took many years for the
city to start building back better – and bigger – and taking on the more recognizable
forms that have come to distinguish it, including, eventually, its famed skyscrapers.
Although rebuilding did begin very soon after the fire, few changes were evident in
the first few years. Most new buildings were still made of wood, initially going up

much as they were before – densely packed, no more than four or five stories – and efforts to enact new building codes faced resistance from property owners.[140] It would seem that in the disaster's immediate aftermath, few if any lessons were learned.

In the following decade, however – particularly after another fire in 1874 destroyed part of the rebuilt (wooden) downtown, and, importantly, after the economy rebounded from the Panic of 1873 that had significantly slowed postfire recovery – Chicago would begin to rise from the ruins in earnest.[141] Slowly and steadily at first, but gaining traction after a few years, monumental changes came to the once wood-paved, diminutively skylined city, where incongruity characterized the urban landscape and humans and farm animals commingled in the streets. Now, taller buildings were erected, new architectural styles were introduced, and new building codes in the fire zone called for the use of fireproof materials. Rather than wood, structures in downtown now comprised stone, brick, marble, and/or steel frames. Many of these were also encased in terracotta, which allowed for exteriors that were both fireproof and exquisitely ornamented, adding to the city's increasingly unique architecture and urban landscape.

Steel-framed buildings were another new technology that eventually allowed for the construction in 1885 of the ten-story Home Insurance Building (demolished in 1931), commonly regarded as the world's first skyscraper.[142] The new rules and materials presented challenges for many, however. Poor and working-class people who could not afford to build with the more expensive fireproof materials now required in downtown, or who could not afford fire insurance, were slowly pushed out of the city center. Yet this migration to the city's outskirts would contribute to the rapid growth of new communities beyond the fire zone.[143] At the time of the fire, Chicago was a city of about 300,000 people spread across roughly 93 square kilometers (36 square miles). By 1890, less than twenty years after the blaze, its population had exceeded 1 million and the area within its boundaries had expanded to 438 square kilometers (169 square miles).[144] In 1893, the city held the World's Columbian Exposition. "One of the most popular and successful of all modern world's fairs, it

---

[140] Smith, *Chicago's Great Fire*, 166, 276–9; Marks, "'Chicago Shall Rise Again.'"

[141] The Panic of 1873 was a financial crisis that led to economic depression in Europe (where it began) and North America for much of the rest of the decade. Marks, "'Chicago Shall Rise Again'"; Bey, "How the Great Fire Changed Chicago Architecture."

[142] Bey, "How the Great Fire Changed Chicago Architecture."

[143] Marks, "'Chicago Shall Rise Again'"; Bey, "How the Great Fire Changed Chicago Architecture."

[144] An annexation of 324 square kilometers (125 square miles) in 1889 "expanded the South Side and made Chicago the second largest and fastest-growing city in the nation." Bachin, *Building the South Side*, 17.

proclaimed for all the world to behold Chicago's full recovery from the fire and its arrival as one of the great metropolises of the world."[145]

Disasters like urban fires can completely transform a city – altering its size, appearance, politics, demographics and social structure, and much else besides. Rather than being merely forces of destruction, they can present opportunities for urban renewal, new and improved building codes, and the creation of disaster-resilient infrastructures. But these changes can come at a cost. Urban reconstruction and renewal too often occur at the expense of the poor and low-income local families forced or priced out of their neighborhoods. After the Chicago Fire, for example, new building codes meant that only the wealthiest could afford to build or purchase in the most resilient and desirable parts of town. Because wood buildings were still permitted outside of the fire zone and, as mentioned, building with fire-resistant materials was so much more expensive, it was the city's poor who lived in Chicago's most vulnerable structures. And this, as we have seen throughout this Element, is only one example of the ways in which vulnerability – and thus disasters – are *created*.

Such lessons matter today perhaps more than ever, nor do they apply only to society's most vulnerable. Human-caused climate change has led to longer wildfire seasons, increased wildfire frequency and severity, and larger burned areas, resulting in part from warmer springs, longer summer dry seasons, and drier soils and vegetation.[146] These fires have already threatened property in affluent rural and suburban areas. During the December 2017 wildfires in Southern California, for instance, the homes of various celebrities (including Oprah Winfrey, Rob Lowe, Ellen Degeneres, and others) came dangerously close to being engulfed by the flames. These encounters are occurring more frequently in part because of where people are choosing to live. "Americans are choosing to build their homes along what's known as the wildland–urban interface [WUI] – the transition zone where woodland and dense vegetation meets human development. Between 1990 and 2010, the number of homes in interface areas grew by 41%," which essentially puts them in or brings them perilously close to high-risk areas.[147]

This is not happening only in the United States, but across the globe. The WUIs in Australia, South Africa, parts of the Mediterranean, and other areas of the world now face heightened wildfire risk as well, as do urban centers in these regions and beyond.[148] Parts of San Diego and Los Angeles in the United States; Catania, Italy; Athens, Greece; Canberra, Australia; Tizi Ouzou, Algeria; Cape

[145] Smith, *Chicago's Great Fire*, 284.
[146] United States Environmental Protection Agency, "Climate Change Indicators: Wildfires."
[147] Cox, "Cities and Suburbs Face Growing Wildfire Threat."
[148] Cutter, Griffin, and Hunt, "A Description and Analysis," 13.

Town, South Africa; and Antalya, Turkey, to name a few, have all suffered major fires in recent years, and the smoke that clouds regional skies can extend for hundreds of miles, affecting towns and cities across large swaths of the planet.

Yet there is another type of disaster that can spread across large regions, or at times even encircle the globe. It can travel with greater fury than a wildfire, leaving behind trails of devastation. Deadly, invisible, and uniquely terrifying, disease epidemics have changed our lives – and our cities – in myriad ways. Section 5 will look at plague, cholera, and COVID-19 to reflect on some of the ways pestilence has influenced the development of the modern city.

5 Pestilence

Among different types of disasters, disease epidemics hold a special status. One could argue that they are the ultimate disaster. One rarely sees disease coming. Its general unpredictability and invisibility make it impossible to seek safer ground. Once established, an epidemic can spread quickly and extensively with the potential to strike down large portions of a population in a relatively short time. It can change an entire society's behavior – isolating individuals, separating loved ones, even pitting family members against one another.

For these reasons and more, the panic and anxiety triggered by the threat of disease is uniquely terrifying. It is a fear of the unknown induced by an invisible killer.[149] Unlike other types of disasters, epidemics cause no direct damage to property – there are no crumbling buildings, no fires, no floods. The diseased cityscape appears manifestly different from what one sees after a cyclone or an earthquake. Yet death hides in every corner. It lurks in people's homes and in the streets; it permeates the very air. A major outbreak can temporarily transform a city into a veritable graveyard, and it often has. The history of epidemics is filled with examples (Figure 6).

Prior to the twentieth century, when most people lived in rural areas and few journeyed very far from their place of birth, the countryside was seen as a safe haven beyond the reach of epidemic disease. Wealthy urban families would notoriously flee the city for their country estates, often leaving behind economic ruin. The idea of disease was thus tied to the city. The city is where disease thrived. Historically, it was filthy. Buildings were packed together; humans lived in close quarters; animals roamed the streets, which reeked of trash and a fusion of human and animal excrement. In humoral understandings of medicine, which dominated from ancient times through the nineteenth century and

---

[149] Ermus, *The Great Plague Scare of 1720*, 3–4.

Figure 6 A plague cityscape. The image depicts the Chevalier Roze
(ca. 1671–1733), a Marseillais nobleman who became well known for various
acts during the plague, among them directing the clearing of corpses from the
Tourette area along the port of Marseille. *Scène de la peste de 1720 à la Tourette*
(*Scene from the Plague of 1720 at la Tourette*), by Catalan-born French painter
Michel Serre (1721), a contemporary eyewitness who captured the horrors of
the 1720 Plague of Provence on canvas. Musée Atger, Montpellier. Getty
Images

beyond, these noxious odors themselves – or miasmas, as they were known –
were believed to be the very cause of disease.[150] Urban areas, especially port
cities, were also considered entryways for disease, where commerce coupled
with vice could result in the introduction of a plague upon humanity.

---

[150] Beginning most notably with Hippocrates (460–377 BCE) and lasting until the late nineteenth
century, when miasmatic explanations of disease etiology were slowly replaced by germ theory,
illness was generally understood to result from the presence of miasmas – disease-causing foul
odors or noxious vapors in the air – that threw off the balance of the four humors (or fluids)
believed to determine all aspects of a person's health and personality. In humoral theory, then,
the cause of disease was not understood as external to the body, like a virus or a bacterium, but
as a state of humoral imbalance. For this reason, treatments or regimens would often emphasize
the elimination of these corrupt vapors (for example, by firing cannons in times of plague) and
the balancing of the humors through practices including bloodletting and purging (for example,
by inducing emesis or employing enemas), as well as the practice of prayer, and/or the use of
stones, talismans, minerals, and brews or concoctions. Such understandings and practices
persisted in Europe, largely unchanged, for centuries. Ermus, "Managing Disaster," 98.

Some of this has changed over the past few centuries. For example, the germ theory of disease has largely replaced earlier understandings of contagion, and cities are now cleaner. Yet the era of travel has allowed for the arrival of pathogens in any and every corner of the world. Few if any villages are so remote that they are completely safe from the reach of epidemic disease. The COVID-19 pandemic has offered many lessons, among them that rural areas today are just as vulnerable as urban ones and can be even more so.[151] It seems that it is not so much about vulnerability of cities as much as it is about vulnerability of gathering – of coming together as people do whether they live in the city or the countryside. Still, the relationship between disease and the city remains significant.

Even if the countryside is no longer as safe as it once may have been (and the extent to which it was is debatable), pathogens are still transported through major urban ports of entry; urban and suburban dwellers still live in closer quarters than in rural areas; the larger concentration of people in the city mean that a disease can spread more quickly than it can beyond the city limits (and therefore wealthy city dwellers still retreat to their country abodes), and so on. Moreover, disease epidemics have had profound effects on the evolution of the world's cities, influencing their layout, institutions, legislation, sanitary practices, culture, and more. In this context, some diseases stand out as particularly ruinous and influential.

One of the deadliest and most notorious diseases in history is plague. Caused by the bacillus *Yersinia pestis*, a bacterium discovered by Alexandre Yersin and, separately, Kitasato Shibasaburō in 1894, plague can take different clinical forms, the most common of which are bubonic, pneumonic, and septicemic. Among these, the bubonic form is the most well known. It is communicated from rodents to humans through the bites of infected fleas and is characterized by its infamous "marks of contagion" – the buboes, or swollen lymph nodes at the armpits and/or groins, the *charbons* or ulcers on the surface of the skin, or the gangrene in one's extremities (the symptom that eventually inspired the name Black Death).[152] The pneumonic form infects the lungs and results either when a person inhales infectious droplets in the air or when the bacteria in bubonic or septicemic cases spreads to the lungs. Finally, the less common septicemic form is an infection of the blood, which makes it especially lethal and can result in rashes on the skin.

---

[151] As with other types of disasters, rural areas – where, among other factors, access to large, well-equipped hospitals is limited or nonexistent – may in fact suffer disproportionately in times of disease.

[152] Studies have also introduced the possibility that human ectoparasites (including body lice and human fleas) had a role to play in transmission of the disease.

Like the bubonic form, it spreads through the bites of infected ectoparasites and is not transmissible from person to person (except by direct contact with contaminated fluid or tissue).

Before the advent of penicillin in 1928, plague was one of the world's greatest pathogenic killers, recurrently popping up in different parts of the globe over a period of centuries. Today, it is ingrained in popular culture and lexicon, recognized as a uniquely dreadful disease, with the Black Death of the fourteenth century its most well-known manifestation. Yet the plague reemerged regularly well beyond the fourteenth century, and, although antibiotics have helped shape understandings of plague as a disease of the past, it endures, emerging periodically in different parts of the world. In the western United States, for example, it persists among rodent populations and leaps into human hosts every so often.

Disease epidemics, particularly outbreaks of plague, have been the driving force behind some of the world's most revolutionary urban transformations, prompting the development of public health practices, technologies, and institutions to prevent their spread that have changed our cities in enduring ways. In 1423, in response to recurring plague outbreaks that began with the Black Death of the mid-fourteenth century, the Republic of Venice constructed the world's first permanent lazaretto or quarantine station, the Lazzaretto Vecchio, on the island of Santa Maria di Nazareth.[153] Institutions like this – meant to isolate ships and sick (or potentially sick) travelers for a period of time before granting them admission to port – were soon established in cities across the Italian Peninsula and Europe in the name of public health. Although the idea of isolating the sick existed before the Black Death, the pandemic also led to the world's first forty-day quarantine or *quarantena* as such,[154] as well as the world's first health pass for traveling in times of disease.[155] Today, the use of both quarantines and documentations of health (such as vaccine cards) remain central, particularly in times of public health crises. Plague outbreaks in Europe also resulted in the removal of plague burial pits and cemeteries outside of the city, as well as the creation of permanent health offices or bureaus. Here again, Italian city-states led the way, burying their plague dead beyond city walls by the mid-to-late fifteenth century,[156] and establishing *magistrati di sanità* (health

---

[153] Stevens Crawshaw, *Plague Hospitals*, 20; Henderson, *Florence under Siege*, 9.

[154] Credit for the first temporary plague hospital and health office goes to the city of Dubrovnik, once known as Ragusa, which developed the concept of quarantine legislation earlier, in 1377, some twenty years after its independence from the Republic of Venice. See Tomić and Blažina, *Expelling the Plague*, 106–7, 110; Henderson, *Florence under Siege*, 9. For more on the forty-day quarantine, see also Stevens Crawshaw, *Plague Hospitals*, 7–8.

[155] Bamji, "Health Passes, Print and Public Health," 441–2; Cipolla, *Public Health*, 29.

[156] "This was in contrast to the normal system where the dead were buried in their own parish, and indeed also differed from countries north of the Alps, such as England, where many plague victims continued to be buried in their local cemeteries." Henderson, *Florence under Siege*, 40, 3–4.

magistracies) in their port cities and other important points of entry. Over the course of the sixteenth century in particular, all the foremost cities of northern Italy had established one of these permanent public health offices. Over time, they increasingly expanded their control, combining legislative, judicial, and executive powers in issues concerning public health, including, as historian Carlo Cipolla observed, "the recording of deaths, burials, the marketing of food, the sewage system, the disposal of byproducts of various economic activities, the hospitals, the hostelries, prostitution, and so on."[157] In this way, northern Italy – the cities of Venice, Florence, Milan, Genoa, and others – became "the most developed area in Europe in regard to health organization."[158] By the eighteenth century, health offices like these could be found in cities all over Europe, forming an important network for monitoring and communicating about all matters pertaining to public health. By this time, too, as I have argued elsewhere, Europe's centralized health offices, such as the *Conseil de Santé* in Paris or the *Junta de Sanidad* in Madrid – both created in response to the Plague of Provence of 1720 – had become important tools of the centralizing state.[159] Disease epidemics, especially those of plague, allowed for the increased regulation and surveillance of everyday life and movements that far outlasted any individual outbreak.

The immediate, more short-term effects of an urban outbreak of plague are no less noteworthy. A major epidemic could bring entire regions to their knees for extended periods of time, significantly interrupting quotidian life across society. One of the last outbreaks of plague in Western Europe, the Plague of Provence (or Plague of Marseille), emerged in the port city of Marseille, then spread across the region of Provence and parts of Languedoc, where it raged, in waves, for two years from 1720 to 1722 and took as many as 126,000 lives.[160] In this time, government and public health officials imposed extensive, strict emergency measures to help bring a stop to the infection and to prevent it from spreading further. Measures included quarantines of varying lengths, social distancing and isolation, strict curfews, trade restrictions and embargoes, the rounding up of beggars and others believed to harbor pestilential odors (miasmas), and the regulation of markets and tighter surveillance and restrictions on smuggling practices. Movement too was restricted and enforced in a number of ways, for example, through amplified

---

[157] Cipolla, *Fighting the Plague*, 3–4. "The minor cities and the rural communities set up health boards only in time of emergency. Both the permanent boards of the major cities and the temporary boards of the minor communities were subordinate and directly answerable to the central health Magistracies of their respective capitals." Ibid., 4.

[158] Ibid., 5. Ermus, *The Great Plague Scare of 1720*, chapter 2.

[159] Ermus, *The Great Plague Scare of 1720*, 72.   [160] Ibid., 1, 43.

surveillance and police presence; the use of certificates of health; the establishment of military cordons (*cordons sanitaires*) made up of armed guards; and the construction of plague walls (which would eventually result in the *mur de la peste* that one can still see in parts of Provence today).

Moreover, dogs and cats were slaughtered (eliminating the rat vector's most prominent predators), and the disposal of trash and human or animal waste in the streets or common walkways was forbidden, as was the keeping of hogs – all of which were believed to emit harmful, disease-causing miasmas. Relatedly, brothels, inns, and taverns were shuttered because it was believed both that God could punish the populace for its sins with disease, and that drinking alcohol could keep the drinker "in continued heat," making them more susceptible to infection.[161]

In fact, all festivals, social events, and large gatherings were forbidden with the exception of religious gatherings to atone for the sins of the people. Ecclesiastical authorities designated prayer days and organized religious processions, and participation was considered mandatory. Essentially, during the Plague of Provence, as during other significant plague outbreaks, quotidian urban life came to a complete standstill. And these measures were not limited to the plague. Although many were created in response to plague epidemics during the centuries-long Second Plague Pandemic that began with the Black Death, they represent a set of tools that would be used over and over in times of infection.[162]

Nor were such plague-time measures wielded only in affected towns or regions. During the Plague of Provence, restrictions like these were introduced not only in southeastern France, where the outbreak raged but across Europe, where neighboring states imposed extensive public health controls to prevent the spread of the infection into their own territories both on the continent and in the overseas colonies.[163] Like other disasters explored here, epidemics are transnational, with ramifications that extend across time and space.

---

[161] *Daily Courant* (London), November 1, 1721, issue 6250. In humoral theory, excessive heat (or, indeed, anything in excess) was believed to throw off one's humoral balance, which could lead to illness.

[162] The First Plague Pandemic, also known as the Plague of Justinian, lasted from the sixth century to the eighth century CE; the Second Plague Pandemic began with the Black Death of the fourteenth century and lasted through much of the nineteenth century. Finally, the Third Plague Pandemic began in mid-nineteenth-century China and lasted through the early-to-mid-twentieth century. For possible thirteenth-century epidemiological origins of the Black Death, see Green, "The Four Black Deaths." For more on the three pandemics, see Snowden, *Epidemics and Society*, chapter 3.

[163] Ermus, *The Great Plague Scare of 1720*, passim.

This is certainly true of cholera, a bacterial, waterborne infection that has been called "the classic epidemic disease of the nineteenth century."[164] Nearly 100 years after the Plague of Provence, a major outbreak emerged in the Ganges Delta of India's West Bengal. It began in 1817 when it struck the city of Calcutta and the rest of Bengal. Within months, it reached Delhi, Bombay (Mumbai), and cities and villages across the Indian subcontinent. In the years that followed, it spread to parts of Asia, the Indian Ocean islands, and the African coast, traveling by both land and sea and "closely linked to trade and to warfare."[165] The First Cholera Pandemic of 1817–26 was only the first of seven to circle much of the globe from the nineteenth to the twenty-first centuries.[166]

For more than 200 years, cholera has terrorized populations and earned a place among the most ghastly diseases known to humans. After an incubation period lasting anywhere from roughly fourteen hours to five days, the victim is suddenly struck with explosive diarrhea – referred to as "rice water stool" because of its watery, white appearance – followed by acute cramps in the legs and feet and at times in other body parts. After one to two days, the second stage sets in, characterized by collapse and continued diarrhea and vomiting that lead to rapid dehydration and ruptured capillaries – the cause behind cholera's notorious effects on the sufferer's appearance: sunken eyes, hollow cheeks, and wrinkled, black-and-blue skin that is cold and clammy to the touch (Figure 7).

> Blood pressure falls, a pulse cannot be felt at the wrist, and urine is suppressed. Violent convulsions of the leg and stomach muscles can cause terrible pain. Loss of liquid is often so great that blood can run as thickly as tar, and the opening of a vein produces no results. Meanwhile, the patient suffers from the horror of full awareness of her or his plight. By this time the patient may have lost most body fluids. Without fluid replacement, death can occur from circulatory or kidney failure. In the worst cases, a healthy person can be dead in hours.[167]

---

[164] Rosenberg, *The Cholera Years*, 1; Arnold, "Cholera and Colonialism in British India," 118.

[165] Echenberg, *Africa in the Time of Cholera*, 17–18. Cholera had been geographically isolated prior to 1817, "but transportation advances, the growth of trade, and rapid urbanization helped it travel quickly out of Asia for the first time." Altschuler, "The Gothic Origins of Global Health," 562.

[166] The Second Pandemic of cholera lasted from 1828 to 1836, the Third Pandemic from 1839 to 1861, the Fourth Pandemic from 1863 to 1879, the Fifth Pandemic from 1881 to 1896, the Sixth Pandemic from 1899 to 1947, and the Seventh Pandemic from 1961 to the present day. Sources provide different years for the pandemics – not atypical in the history of epidemics since periodization depends on a number of factors including where, geographically, one is looking. I have chosen the years provided in Echenberg's *Africa in the Time of Cholera*. While some authors cut off the Seventh Pandemic in the 1970s, most scholars agree that it is in fact ongoing. See, for example, Chigudu, *The Political Life of an Epidemic*, 184; Hamlin, *Cholera*, 4.

[167] Echenberg, *Africa in the Time of Cholera*, 7–8.

Figure 7 An engraving depicting a young woman before and after contracting cholera. The disease acts quickly, causing its victims to have sunken eyes and to appear blue from dehydration (hence its nickname, "the blue death"). The Italian description on the left reads, "Young Viennese woman of 26 years"; on the right it reads, "The same woman an hour after the invasion of the cholera, and four hours before her death." Italy, engraving with watercolor, circa 1831. Wellcome Collection, no. 5396i. Public Domain 1.0

Those who survive this stage see an end to the purging and the accompanying symptoms. Their chances of survival rise dramatically, yet the risk of death within a few days remains if kidney function was severely impaired.[168]

The disease would soon become endemic in regions around the world, where it continues to pose a threat to both local communities and travelers. As with most if not all epidemics – we have seen with COVID-19 just how difficult it is to obtain accurate numbers of infections and deaths even today – it is impossible to know how many have died during any of the cholera pandemics. Estimates abound, but few are backed by sufficient evidence. According to historian Christopher Hamlin, records for India and Pakistan, where cholera was endemic, "represent a reasonable degree of institutional continuity." These report 22 million deaths from 1877 to 1954, "with decadal cholera mortality rising as high as 1.5/1,000 in 1887–96, equivalent to 429,000 average annual cholera deaths."[169]

---

[168] Ibid.

[169] Hamlin, *Cholera*, 3. For numerous additional estimates covering the First Pandemic through the Sixth, see Echenberg, *Africa in the Time of Cholera*, 15–28.

More recent numbers for Africa and Haiti are instructive. Today, Africa accounts for at least 90 percent of the world's total number of cholera cases and deaths. In 2009, for example, Africa's 217,000 cases represented 98 percent of the global total (221,000).[170] During its catastrophic epidemic of 2008 to 2009, Zimbabwe alone saw more than 98,000 infections and more than 4,000 deaths in what has been called the "largest and most extensive" cholera outbreak in Africa's recorded history.[171]

Haiti, meanwhile, did not know the horrors of cholera until United Nations peacekeeping forces introduced it on the island in the aftermath of the earthquake. In the first three years after the arrival of the disease in October 2010, Haiti saw more than 638,000 cases and nearly 8,000 deaths. Since then, the numbers have declined each year, but not before infecting upward of 820,000 people and taking nearly 10,000 lives.[172] Given that cholera is treatable by rehydration therapy and, in severe cases, antibiotics, it is worth noting that such ongoing deaths in these parts of the world and others are the result of poverty and (neo)colonialism no less than of disease.

Although not nearly as deadly as plague once was (that is, before antibiotics), cholera too has nevertheless helped transform the city in enduring ways, particularly through its influence on the development of sanitation technology and modern public health. Even if sanitary infrastructures have not been implemented evenly across the globe, their impact on the modern city and on our everyday lives has been nothing short of revolutionary.[173] Beginning most notably in the nineteenth century, outbreaks of cholera and other diseases (such as typhoid) in industrial cities in Britain and across Europe spurred sanitary reforms, including the construction of safe water supplies and municipal sewerage systems.[174]

---

[170] Echenberg, *Africa in the Time of Cholera*, 122.

[171] Chigudu, *The Political Life of an Epidemic*, 1.

[172] Ministère de la Santé Publique et de la Population d'Haïti (MSPP), "Rapport du Réseau National de Surveillance, Choléra."

[173] In parts of Africa, for example, "the lessons of the past seem difficult to learn ... [A]lthough preventive public health expenditures for clean water and decent sanitation are cost effective, such measures are not attractive to African politicians or international donors. Instead, millions are spent on emergency relief each time a cholera outbreak careens out of control." Echenberg, *Africa in the Time of Cholera*, 183.

[174] The implementation of hygienic practices to prevent disease – such as cleaning streets, clearing gutters, increasing ventilation, and others – was not new in the nineteenth century. Sanitary practices based on humoral understandings of medicine were employed during earlier outbreaks of plague and other diseases. For example, yellow fever outbreaks in late eighteenth-century Philadelphia spurred efforts "to have the streets properly cleansed and purified by the scavengers [people hired to clean the streets], and all the filth immediately hawled [*sic*] away." However, it was in the nineteenth century that these efforts resulted in the kinds of larger-scale sanitary infrastructures we recognize today. Carey, *A Short Account of the Malignant Fever*, 21.

Other global cities soon began to follow suit. By the 1860s and 1870s, for example, some of India's largest urban centers began implementing large-scale sanitary improvements, which significantly lowered urban mortality rates. Calcutta, which had suffered between 2,500 and 7,000 deaths from cholera every year between 1841 and 1865, saw those numbers decline dramatically after the opening of a new sewage system in 1865 and the introduction of a filtered water supply in 1869. Enhanced water supplies in the cities of Bombay and Madras would soon have similar results. Yet such critical urban innovations would do little to improve conditions for the smaller towns and villages of India, where a lack of clean water and sanitation meant that cholera remained a constant threat.[175]

Other infectious diseases have had similarly monumental effects on cities. Over the course of the twentieth and twenty-first centuries, epidemics of measles, diphtheria, SARS (severe acute respiratory syndrome), MERS (Middle East respiratory syndrome), tuberculosis, various influenzas, COVID-19, and others have helped drive initiatives to ensure clean water supplies, increase ventilation in housing and public buildings, de-densify urban housing, and other developments (Figure 8). The New York State Tenement House Act of 1901, for example, was among the first in the United States to prohibit the construction of dark, unventilated tenement buildings. It required that city buildings have exterior windows, adequate ventilation and square footage, indoor bathrooms, and fire escapes.[176] Such changes served to significantly reduce the number of infections and disease-related deaths in urban areas. Yet our cities today are not completely safe from epidemic disease – quite the contrary.

The COVID-19 pandemic laid bare the vulnerability of city dwellers to infectious disease outbreaks. Population density and overcrowding; a lack of indoor ventilation; an absence of hand-washing stations, of pedestrian-friendly green and open spaces, and in much of the world, of potable water and waste management; a continued need for public transportation; the near nonexistence of self-sufficient cities that need not rely on the importation of food and other goods from around the globe – all of these factors and more contribute to our global cities' vulnerability to epidemics and pandemics. What, then, can the cities of the world do to reduce this exposure to the universe of diseases that exist on our planet?

Our cities may need to be erected or repurposed with our biological vulnerability in mind, taking into account both our physical and psychological health. During COVID-19, cities such as Oakland, New York, Calgary, Cologne, and others closed some of their streets to provide pedestrians added space. In many

---

[175] Arnold, *Colonizing the Body*, 166–7.

[176] Batlan, "Gender and the Rise of the Welfare State," 93; Social Welfare History Project (VCU Libraries), "Tenement House Reform."

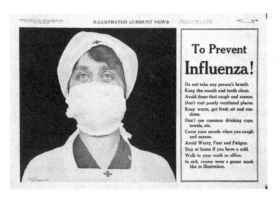

Figure 8 Public health poster "To prevent influenza!" The photograph depicts
a Red Cross nurse with a gauze mask over her nose and mouth. The text provides
tips to prevent infection, including good hygiene, proper ventilation, staying home,
and wearing a mask. Black-and-white poster. Paul Thompson (photographer). New
Haven, CT.: *Illustrated Current News*, 1918. Courtesy of the National Library of
Medicine Digital Collections, http://resource.nlm.nih.gov/101580385

cases, these changes were temporary, but we may consider longer-term investments in added green and open spaces and greenbelts that promote safely
getting outside and thus physical and mental health.

Our homes and workplaces will also need to be brighter, better ventilated, and
more energy and heat efficient. Too many office buildings, for example, lack
operable windows, potentially causing pathogens to be sealed in and recirculated.
The construction of outdoor hand-washing stations or of additional elevators and
staircases to help reduce "pinch points" that bring people too close to one another
could also help make our cities safer both in times of disease and of health. The
pandemic-resilient city will also be better able to detect diseases and track
infections through such methods as wastewater surveillance.[177]

Such cities will need to be more localized, sustainable, and self-sufficient
than their current non-resilient counterparts. Mass public transportation, for
instance, is a high-risk endeavor during an epidemic (despite its benefits for the
environment). Perhaps making everyday needs and services more accessible –
say, a fifteen- or twenty-minute walk or bike ride away (what has been called the
fifteen- or twenty-minute city or neighborhood) – could alleviate the need to
regularly travel longer distances.[178]

---

[177] Consider, for example, the Underworlds project of the Senseable City Lab and Alm Lab at MIT.
As described on the project website, "Underworlds imagines a future in which sewage is mined
for real-time information. Insights on eating habits, genetic tendencies, drug consumption,
contagious diseases, and overall health lie in the sewage system."

[178] Constable, "How Do You Build a City for a Pandemic?"; Moreno et al., "Introducing the '15-
Minute City.'"

The COVID-19 pandemic also exposed our overreliance on the global food supply chain. Not only do interruptions of the supply chains result in empty shelves, but the global transport of food can only facilitate the rapid circulation of pathogens around the world. Sourcing more of our food from local farms can help ensure a supply of fresh food while also supporting the local economy and reducing our impact on the environment. In fact, some of these suggestions may assist not only in reducing our vulnerability to epidemic disease, but in lessening the impact of another one of the defining challenges of our age: human-caused climate change.

6 Conclusion: Climate Change and the Future of Cities

The most recent assessment report of the Intergovernmental Panel on Climate Change (IPCC) – the body of the United Nations dedicated to assessing the science related to climate change – noted that "climate change is widespread, rapid, and intensifying, and some trends are now irreversible."[179] Global warming is leading to more heat waves and longer warm seasons, as well as shorter cold seasons and stronger snowstorms. Some parts of the world have seen more intense rains and flooding, while others are confronting an increase in drought and desertification. The oceans of the world are also getting warmer and seeing reduced oxygen levels, as well as an increase in acidification (which occurs as the ocean absorbs more carbon dioxide from the atmosphere). Meanwhile, the polar regions of the earth are warming faster than anywhere else, causing permafrost to thaw, glaciers and ice sheets to melt, and the loss of seasonal snow cover.[180]

The associated acceleration of sea level rise as a result of anthropogenic climate change threatens more than 100 million people per year and places dense coastal development and major regional infrastructures at risk. Sea level rise can also elevate water tables along coasts and cause increased flooding "from a combination of groundwater emergence and increased discharge rates."[181] Land subsidence too – often caused by human activity such as groundwater extraction – threatens to inundate coastal cities around the globe even sooner than sea level rise models predict. Primarily in coastal cities of South, Southeast, and East Asia where the most rapid subsidence is occurring,

---

[179] United Nations, "IPCC Report"; IPCC, "Sixth Assessment Report."

[180] Short and Farmer, "Cities and Climate Change," 1038.

[181] Hirschfeld, Hill, and Plane, "Adapting to Sea Level Rise," 636–7.

> After a period of approximately 2,000 years of little change, global average sea level rose throughout the 20th century, and the rate of change has accelerated in recent years. When averaged over all of the world's oceans, absolute sea level has risen at an average rate of 0.06 inches per year from 1880 to 2013. Since 1993, however, average sea level has risen at a rate of 0.12 to 0.14 inches per year – roughly twice as fast as the long-term trend.

United States Environmental Protection Agency, "Climate Change Indicators: Sea Level."

but also along the coasts of North America, Europe, Africa, and Australia, land is subsiding faster than sea level is rising, which will lead to severe flood events much sooner than expected.[182]

In short, we are entering what many have called a new climate (or climatic) regime.[183] The coastal cities of the world, home to a growing majority of the world's urban population, are increasingly at risk. As historian Ted Steinberg has noted,

> The sea is knocking at the doors of coastal cities all across the world. From the bustle of New York to the canals of Amsterdam, from the shopping malls of Guangzhou to the slums of Mumbai, from Kolkata to Kuala Lumpur, London to Lima, the water is rising and perennial inundations are running up quite a bill, estimated to be roughly $6 billion a year in the 136 largest coastal cities.[184]

Despite the dangers and financial costs of remaining apathetic, however, urban areas are generally not acting quickly enough toward mitigating or adapting to the effects of climate change and rising seas. Instead, decision makers have been slow to "move beyond vulnerability assessments" and begin adapting their communities to the threat of sea level rise and the possibility of more frequently occurring extreme weather events.[185] Compared to rural areas, cities have easier access to the resources necessary to make changes

---

[182]   Wu, Wei, and D'Hondt, "Subsidence in Coastal Cities," 1. Discussing the disastrous 2022 floods in Pakistan, UN Secretary-General António Guterres referred to South Asia as a "climate crisis hotspot" where "people were 15 times more likely to die from climate impacts." He continued, "Today, it's Pakistan. Tomorrow, it could be your country." Fraser, "Pakistan Floods."

[183]   Short and Farmer, "Cities and Climate Change," 1038. One of the earliest recorded mentions of the phrase "new climate regime" appears in a 1976 hearing before the United States Congress, which reads, "There is growing evidence that the world is entering a new climate regime. Both the rate of change of the climate and the amplitude of short period climatic variations will be much more pronounced." United States Congress, House Committee on Science and Technology, *The National Climate Program Act*, 433. One of the earlier, if not earliest, mentions of "new *climatic* regime" appears in the January 17, 1890, issue of the *Saint Paul Daily Globe*:

> It used to be that a mild winter on this hemisphere produced an opposite effect on the other hemisphere. But like all other old ideas, this one has passed away, and we are living under an entirely *new climatic regime* [italics added]. What are the causes of this modification of the conditions governing the temperature of the whole world? Has our orb moved into a new place in space? Or is the earth for any reason being subjected to a greater amount of heat, and, if so, what are the reasons? "Snowless Winters," *Saint Paul Daily Globe*, January 17, 1890.

For more recent mentions, see, among others, the work of Bruno Latour, including his books *Facing Gaia* and *Down to Earth*.

[184]   Steinberg, "Afterword," 184.
[185]   Hirschfeld, Hill, and Plane, "Adapting to Sea Level Rise," 636.

toward increasing resilience, most important among these capital, political clout, and at times the country's (or even the world's) attention. Yet numerous challenges remain, particularly for the poorer, and often most vulnerable, regions of the world, some of which, moreover, are responsible for a large share of the pollution.

Adapting cities and infrastructure to climate change requires significant investments of money, time, research, energy, and commitment, and for many municipal governments, confronting and tackling their city's climate-change-related vulnerabilities may not be a priority. Working to increase water supplies and decrease water demand to prevent drought, for example, or reducing the number of impermeable surfaces to reduce flood risk, requires extensive planning, funding, and time.[186] But for cities that lack the necessary resources to rise to the challenge or that have not yet begun to feel the most deleterious effects of climate change, or for leaders to whom the threat of climate change seems far off or even a fiction – after all, the slow disaster of rising seas does not happen overnight – such investments will not be of primary concern.

Tackling some of these more fundamental obstacles to increasing resilience – indifference, lack of funding, and misinformation – will require the concentrated, concerted efforts of countries, cities, organizations, and individuals around the world. And here, there is reason for hope. Cities are simultaneously largely responsible for climate change, most at risk of suffering from its effects, and most capable of lessening its impacts on humans and the environment.[187] Recent years have seen the formation of various initiatives and collaborations aimed directly at combating climate change and reducing its effects on communities and the environment. Some are occurring at the global level, a notable example of which is the C40 Cities network, which consists of ninety-six members from across the globe. Their primary objectives include halving the emissions of their member cities within a decade, "while improving equity, building resilience, and creating the conditions for everyone, everywhere to thrive" and supporting "cities around the world to create and implement climate action plans in line with the 1.5°C target of the Paris Agreement."[188] In 2020, when the Paris Climate Accords proved fragile with the withdrawal of the United States (under the administration of Donald Trump), the city-based initiative served as a meaningful reminder that many of the largest metropolises

---

[186] Short and Farmer, "Cities and Climate Change," 1041.

[187] Although cities account for less than 2 percent of the earth's surface, they consume 78 percent of the world's energy and produce more than 60 percent of greenhouse gas emissions. United Nations, "Cities."

[188] C40 Cities Climate Leadership Group, "About C40."

of the world, including those of the United States, could and would nevertheless remain committed to the principles and ambitions of the Agreement.

Other initiatives are occurring at the national and local levels, and they are no less noteworthy. In anticipation of a hotter and wetter climate, the city of Chicago, for example, has committed to planting more trees, to offering tax incentives for installing cooling, green garden roofs on office buildings, and notably, to repaving its roads with permeable materials that allow water to filter through to the soil.[189] Cities around the globe are also working toward becoming cleaner and more sustainable by limiting traffic, expanding pedestrian areas and bike lanes, constructing green buildings, and electrifying mass transit, among other initiatives. Cities like Copenhagen, Singapore, Vancouver, Vienna, and others have been global leaders in the municipal sustainability movement, and Santiago de Chile is now "home to the largest fleet of electric buses outside of China."[190] Although more must be done to slow the warming of the planet – indeed, the situation seems increasingly urgent – these examples and many more point to a growing interest in reducing our carbon footprint and in both combating and increasing our resilience to the effects of climate change.

Growing up in the 1980s, I regularly heard about a different environmental crisis – the depletion of the ozone layer. The discovery in the 1980s that the protective layer of gas that absorbs harmful ultraviolet radiation from the sun was due to disappear in the following decades caused worldwide alarm and led to the adoption in 1987 of the Montreal Protocol on Substances that Deplete the Ozone Layer – an international environmental agreement that regulated "the production and consumption of nearly 100 man-made chemicals referred to as ozone depleting substances (ODS) ... Adopted on 15 September 1987, the Protocol is to date the only UN treaty ever that has been ratified [in] every country on Earth."[191] Today, as the ozone layer slowly recovers, the landmark agreement serves as a model example of what the world can achieve when it comes together under a common cause.[192] From where we stand, the road to combating climate change seems long and the challenges daunting, but collective action has worked before, and it may well work again. In fact, it must. It may be our only hope.

---

[189] Short and Farmer, "Cities and Climate Change," 1041.

[190] C40 Cities Climate Leadership Group, "From Pilots to Scale."

[191] UN Environmental Programme, "The Montreal Protocol."   [192] Reiny, "NASA Study."

Bibliography

Archives

Library of Congress, Digital Collections.

National Library of Medicine, Digital Collections.

New Orleans Public Library, City Archives (NOPL). Alphabetical and Chronological Digest of the Acts & Deliberations of the Cabildo, 1769–1803: A Record of the Spanish Government in New Orleans.

Williams Research Center (WRC), Colonial Louisiana Newspaper Collection.

Published Sources

Acosta, Rolando J., Nishant Kishore, Rafael A. Irizarry, and Caroline O. Buckee. "Quantifying the Dynamics of Migration after Hurricane Maria in Puerto Rico." *PNAS* 117, no. 51 (December 2020): 32772–8.

Altschuler, Sari. "The Gothic Origins of Global Health." *American Literature* 89, no. 3 (September 2017): 557–90.

Alvarez, Lizette. "A Great Migration from Puerto Rico Is Set to Transform Orlando." *New York Times*. November 17, 2017. www.nytimes.com/2017/11/17/us/puerto-ricans-orlando.html.

Amri, Ikhwan, and Sri Rum Giyarsih. "Monitoring Urban Physical Growth in Tsunami-Affected Areas: A Case Study of Banda Aceh City, Indonesia." *GeoJournal* (January 2021). https://doi.org/10.1007/s10708-020-10362-6.

Arnold, David. "Cholera and Colonialism in British India." *Past & Present* 113, no. 1 (November 1986): 118–51.

Arnold, David. *Colonizing the Body: State Medicine and Epidemic Disease in Nineteenth-Century India*. Berkeley: University of California Press, 1993.

Aspinall, Edward. *Islam and Nation: Separatist Rebellion in Aceh, Indonesia*. Stanford, CA: Stanford University Press, 2009.

Aswathanarayana, U. "Overview and Integration of Part 4." In *The Indian Ocean Tsunami*, edited by Tad S. Murty, U. Aswathanarayana, and Niru Nirupama. London: CRC Press, 2007, pp. 405–8.

Azevedo, João, Sandra Serrano, and Carlos S. Oliveira. "The Next 1755: Myth and Reality. Priorities and Actions to Develop in Case of an Earthquake in the Lisbon Metropolitan Area." In *The 1755 Lisbon Earthquake: Revisited*, edited by Luiz A. Mendes-Victor, Carlos Sousa Oliveira, João Azevedo, and António Ribeiro. New York: Springer, 2009, pp. 559–79.

Bachin, Robin F. *Building the South Side: Urban Space and Civic Culture in Chicago, 1890–1919*. Chicago, IL: University of Chicago Press, 2004.

Bamji, Alexandra. "Health Passes, Print and Public Health in Early Modern Europe." *Social History of Medicine* 32, No. 3 (August 2019): 441–64.

Barragán, Juan Manuel, and María de Andrés. "Analysis and Trends of the World's Coastal Cities and Agglomerations." *Ocean & Coastal Management* 114 (2015): 11–20.

Batlan, Felice. "Gender and the Rise of the Welfare State in Fin-de-Siècle New York City: The Case of the Tenement Regulation." In *The Legal Tender of Gender: Law, Welfare, and the Regulation of Women's Poverty*, edited by Shelley A. M. Gavigan and Dorothy E. Chunn. Oxford: Hart, 2010, pp. 75–102.

Bavel, Bas van, Daniel R. Curtis, Jessica Dijkman et al. *Disasters and History: The Vulnerability and Resilience of Past Societies*. Cambridge: Cambridge University Press, 2020.

Bey, Lee. "How the Great Fire Changed Chicago Architecture." *Chicago Sun Times*. October 8, 2021. https://chicago.suntimes.com/2021/10/8/22677929/how-great-chicago-fire-changed-chicago-architecture.

Birkmann, Joern. "Risk and Vulnerability Indicators at Different Scales: Applicability, Usefulness and Policy Implications." *Environmental Hazards* 7 (2007): 20–31.

Bullard, Robert D. *Dumping in Dixie: Race, Class, and Environmental Quality*. New York: Routledge, 2000.

C40 Cities Climate Leadership Group. "About C40." *C40 Cities*. 2022. www.c40.org/about-c40.

C40 Cities Climate Leadership Group. "From Pilots to Scale: Lessons from Electric Bus Deployments in Santiago de Chile." *C40 Knowledge Hub*. June 2020. www.c40knowledgehub.org/s/article/From-Pilots-to-Scale-Lessons-from-Electric-Bus-Deployments-in-Santiago-de-Chile?language=en_US.

Carey, Mathew. *A Short Account of the Malignant Fever, Lately Prevalent in Philadelphia: With a Statement of the Proceedings That Took Place on the Subject in Different Parts of the United States*. Philadelphia, PA: Printed by the author, 1793.

Carp, Benjamin L. "Fire of Liberty: Firefighters, Urban Voluntary Culture, and the Revolutionary Movement." *William and Mary Quarterly* 58 (2001): 781–818.

Casselman, Ben. "Katrina Washed Away New Orleans's Black Middle Class." *FiveThirtyEight*. August 24, 2015. https://fivethirtyeight.com/features/katrina-washed-away-new-orleanss-black-middle-class.

Cheng, Margaret Harris. "Health and Housing after the Indian Ocean Tsunami." *Lancet* 369, no. 9579 (June 2007): 2066–8.

"CHEER UP," *Chicago Tribune*. October 11, 1871. www.chicagotribune.com/news/ct-great-chicago-fire-cheer-up-editorial-20210820-f2emncydkzg45arl4xx6ektrpe-story.html.

Chigudu, Simukai. *The Political Life of an Epidemic: Cholera, Crisis and Citizenship in Zimbabwe*. Cambridge: Cambridge University Press, 2020.

Cipolla, Carlo M. *Fighting the Plague in Seventeenth-Century Italy*. Madison: University of Wisconsin Press, 1981.

Cipolla, Carlo M. *Public Health and the Medical Profession in the Renaissance*. Cambridge: Cambridge University Press, 1976.

Cobb, Jelani. "Race and the Storm." *The New Yorker*. August 16, 2015. www.newyorker.com/magazine/2015/08/24/race-and-the-storm.

Constable, Harriet. "How Do You Build a City for a Pandemic?" *BBC Future*. April 26, 2020. www.bbc.com/future/article/20200424-how-do-you-build-a-city-for-a-pandemic.

Courtney, Chris. *The Nature of Disaster in China: The 1931 Yangzi River Flood*. Cambridge: Cambridge University Press, 2018.

Courtney, Chris. "Picturing Disaster: The 1931 Wuhan Flood." *China Dialogue*. September 11, 2018. www.chinadialogue.net/culture/10811-Picturing-disaster-The-1931-Wuhan-flood/en.

Cox, Mark. "Cities and Suburbs Face Growing Wildfire Threat." *MSU Denver RED*. January 25, 2022. https://red.msudenver.edu/2022/cities-and-suburbs-face-growing-wildfire-threat.

Cutter, W. Bowman, Jenny Griffin, and Laurel Hunt. "A Description and Analysis of Mediterranean Cities and Regions Planning for Climate Impacts." *Cities and the Environment* 10, no. 2, article 7 (2018): 1–30. https://digitalcommons.lmu.edu/cate/vol10/iss2/7.

Dan, Maria Bostenaru. "Timber Frame Historic Structures and the Local Seismic Culture: An Argumentation." In *Earthquake Hazard Impact and Urban Planning*, edited by Maria Bostenaru Dan, Iuliana Armas, and Agostino Goretti. Dordrecht: Springer Science & Business Media, 2014, pp. 213–30.

"Disaster, n." *OED Online*. March 2022. Oxford University Press. www-oed-com.libweb.lib.utsa.edu/view/Entry/53561?rskey=d33WhK&result=1.

Dubois, Laurent. *Haiti: The Aftershocks of History*. New York: Metropolitan Books, 2012.

Echenberg, Myron. *Africa in the Time of Cholera: A History of Pandemics from 1817 to the Present*. Cambridge: Cambridge University Press, 2011.

Echenique, Martin, and Luis Melgar, "Mapping Puerto Rico's Hurricane Migration with Mobile Phone Data." *Bloomberg City Lab*. May 11, 2018.

www.bloomberg.com/news/articles/2018-05-11/where-puerto-rico-s-resi dents-migrated-since-maria.

Edwards, Jay D. "The Origins of Creole Architecture." *Winterthur Portfolio* 29 (1994): 155–89.

Ermus, Cindy. *The Great Plague Scare of 1720: Disaster and Diplomacy in the Eighteenth-Century Atlantic World.* Cambridge: Cambridge University Press, 2023.

Ermus, Cindy. "Managing Disaster and Understanding Disease and the Environment in the Early Eighteenth Century." In *Disease and the Environment in the Medieval and Early Modern Worlds*, edited by Lori Jones. New York: Routledge, 2022, pp. 91–106.

Ermus, Cindy. "Spanish Foundations of the French Quarter: Rebuilding Colonial New Orleans in the Wake of Disaster." In *Port Cities of the Atlantic World: Sea-Facing Histories of the US South*, edited by Jacob Steere-Williams and Blake C. Scott. Columbia: University of South Carolina Press 2023.

Ewen, Shane. *What Is Urban History?* Cambridge: Polity Press, 2016.

Ferré-Sadurní, Luis, and Anemona Hartocollis. "Maria Strikes, and Puerto Rico Goes Dark." *New York Times.* September 20, 2017. www.nytimes.com/2017/ 09/20/us/hurricane-maria-puerto-rico-power.html.

Fleming, Phoebe. "Why Orlando's Growth Rate Is the Second Fastest of the 30 Largest U.S. Cities." *Orlando Economic Partnership.* January 1, 2021. https:// news.orlando.org/blog/orlandos-fast-growth-in-a-category-all-its-own.

Flores, Antonio, and Jens Manuel Krogstad. "Puerto Rico's Population Declined Sharply after Hurricanes Maria and Irma." *Pew Research Center.* July 26, 2019. www.pewresearch.org/fact-tank/2019/07/26/puerto-rico-popu lation-2018.

Frankenberg, Elizabeth, Jed Friedman, Thomas Gillespie et al. "Mental Health in Sumatra after the Tsunami." *American Journal of Public Health* 98, no. 9 (2008): 1671–7.

Fraser, Simon. "Pakistan Floods Are 'a Monsoon on Steroids,' Warns UN chief." *BBC News.* August 30, 2022. www.bbc.com/news/world-asia-62722117.

Graham, David A. "Trump's Dubious Revisionist History of Hurricane Maria." *The Atlantic.* September 12, 2018. www.theatlantic.com/politics/archive/ 2018/09/trump-hurricane-maria-florence-revisionism/570070.

Green, Monica. "The Four Black Deaths." *American Historical Review* 125, no. 5 (December 2020): 1601–31.

Hamilton, Reeve. "The Huddled Masses: Five Years after Hurricane Katrina, Louisiana Exiles Have Fundamentally Changed Houston, and Vice-Versa."

Texas Tribune. August 30, 2010. www.texastribune.org/2010/08/30/five-years-houstonians-conflicted-about-katrina.

Hamlin, Christopher. *Cholera: The Biography*. Oxford: Oxford University Press, 2009.

Henderson, John. *Florence under Siege: Surviving Plague in an Early Modern City*. New Haven, CT: Yale University Press, 2019.

Hernández, Arelis R., Mark Berman, and John Wagner. "San Juan Mayor Slams Trump Administration Comments on Puerto Rico Hurricane Response." *Washington Post*. September 30, 2017. www.washingtonpost.com/news/post-nation/wp/2017/09/29/san-juan-mayor-slams-trump-administration-comments-on-puerto-rico-hurricane-response.

Hewitt, Kenneth. *Regions of Risk: A Geographical Introduction to Disasters*. New York: Routledge, 1997.

Hinojosa, Jennifer. "Two Sides of the Coin of Puerto Rican Migration: Depopulation in Puerto Rico and the Redefinition of the Diaspora." *CENTRO: Journal of the Center for Puerto Rican Studies* 30, no. 3 (Fall 2018): 230–53.

Hinojosa, Jennifer, and Edwin Meléndez. "Puerto Rican Exodus: One Year since Hurricane Maria." *CENTRO: The Center for Puerto Rican Studies*. September 2018. https://centropr.hunter.cuny.edu/sites/default/files/RB2018-05_SEPT2018%20%281%29.pdf.

Hirschfeld, Daniella, Kristina E. Hill, and Ellen Plane. "Adapting to Sea Level Rise: Insights from a New Evaluation Framework of Physical Design Projects." *Coastal Management* 49, no. 6 (2021): 636–1.

Horowitz, Andy. *Katrina: A History, 1915–2015*. Cambridge, MA: Harvard University Press, 2020.

Horowitz, Andy, and Jacob A. C. Remes. "Introduction: Introducing Critical Disaster Studies." In *Critical Disaster Studies*, edited by Jacob A. C. Remes and Andy Horowitz. Philadelphia: University of Pennsylvania Press, 2021, pp. 1–8.

Hoyos, Joshua. "100 Days after Hurricane Maria, San Juan Mayor Thanks Americans, Slams Trump As 'Disaster-in-Chief'." *ABC News*. December 29, 2017. https://abcnews.go.com/US/100-days-hurricane-maria-san-juan-mayor-americans/story?id=52033032.

Intergovernmental Panel on Climate Change (IPCC). "Sixth Assessment Report." 2021. www.ipcc.ch/assessment-report/ar6.

Jasparro, Christopher, and Jonathan Taylor. "Transnational Geopolitical Competition and Natural Disasters: Lessons from the Indian Ocean Tsunami." In *The Indian Ocean Tsunami: The Global Response to a Natural Disaster*, edited by Pradyumna P. Karan and Shanmugam Subbiah. Lexington: University Press of Kentucky, 2011, pp. 283–99.

Juran, Luke. "Indian Ocean Tsunami, 2004." In *Natural Hazards and Disasters: From Avalanches and Climate Change to Water Spouts and Wildfires, V. 2*, edited by Bimal Kanti Paul. Santa Barbara, CA: ABC-CLIO, 2020, pp. 197–201.

Kar, Nilamadhab, Rameshraj Krishnaraaj, and Kavitha Rameshraj. "Long-Term Mental Health Outcomes following the 2004 Asian Tsunami Disaster: A Comparative Study on Direct and Indirect Exposure." *Disaster Health* 2, no. 1 (Jan.–Mar. 2014): 35–45.

Karan, Pradyumna P. "Introduction: When Nature Turns Savage." In *The Indian Ocean Tsunami: The Global Response to a Natural Disaster*, edited by Pradyumna P. Karan and Shanmugam Subbiah. Lexington: University Press of Kentucky, 2011, pp. 1–31.

Kelman, Ilan. *Disaster by Choice: How Our Actions Turn Natural Hazards into Catastrophes*. Oxford: Oxford University Press, 2020.

Kelman, Ilan. "Natural Disasters Do Not Exist (Natural Hazards Do Not Exist Either)." July 9, 2010, pp. 1–5. www.ilankelman.org/miscellany/NaturalDisasters.doc.

Kerr, Derek N. *Petty Felony, Slave Defiance, and Frontier Villainy: Crime and Criminal Justice in Spanish Louisiana, 1770–1803*. New York: Garland, 1993.

Klein, Naomi. *The Shock Doctrine: The Rise of Disaster Capitalism*. New York: Picador, 2007.

Latour, Bruno. *Down to Earth: Politics in the New Climatic Regime*. Cambridge: Polity Press, 2018.

Latour, Bruno. *Facing Gaia: Eight Lectures on the New Climatic Regime*. Cambridge: Polity Press, 2017.

Loewenstein, Antony. *Disaster Capitalism: Making a Killing out of Catastrophe*. London: Verso, 2015.

Marks, Peter. "'Chicago Shall Rise Again': Rebuilding a Better City after the Blaze." *WTTW*. October 2020. https://interactive.wttw.com/chicago-stories/chicago-fire/chicago-shall-rise-again-rebuilding-a-better-city-after-the-blaze.

McCaughey, Jamie W., Patrick Daly, Ibnu Mundir, Saiful Mahdi, and Anthony Patt. "Socio-economic Consequences of Post-disaster Reconstruction in Hazard-Exposed Areas." *Nature Sustainability* 1 (2018): 38–43.

McGranahan, Gordon, Deborah Balk, and Bridget Anderson. "Low Coastal Zone Settlements." *Tiempo* 59 (April 2006): 23–6.

Meyer, Robinson. "What's Happening with the Relief Effort in Puerto Rico?" *The Atlantic*. October 4, 2017. www.theatlantic.com/science/archive/2017/10/what-happened-in-puerto-rico-a-timeline-of-hurricane-maria/541956.

Milken Institute School of Public Health, George Washington University. "Ascertainment of the Estimated Excess Mortality from Hurricane María in Puerto Rico." August 27, 2018. https://prstudy.publichealth.gwu.edu.

Ministère de la Santé Publique et de la Population d'Haïti (MSPP). "Rapport du Réseau National de Surveillance, Choléra." January 2020. www.mspp .gouv.ht.

Modica, Marco, and Roberto Zoboli. "Vulnerability, Resilience, Hazard, Risk, Damage, and Loss: A Socio-ecological Framework for Natural Disaster Analysis," *Web Ecology* 16 (February 2016): 59–62.

Molesky, Mark. *This Gulf of Fire: The Great Lisbon Earthquake, Or Apocalypse in the Age of Science and Reason.* New York: Vintage Books, 2015.

Moreno, Carlos, Zaheer Allam, Didier Chabaud, Catherine Gall, and Florent Pratlong. "Introducing the '15-Minute City': Sustainability, Resilience, and Place Identity in Future Post-pandemic Cities." *Smart Cities* 4, no. 1 (2021): 93–111.

National Ocean Service, National Oceanic and Atmospheric Administration. "What Is the Difference between a Hurricane and a Typhoon?" February 26, 2021. https://oceanservice.noaa.gov/facts/cyclone.html.

"November 1, 1721." *Daily Courant* (London), issue 6250.

Nowakowski, Kelsey. "Charts Show How Hurricane Katrina Changed New Orleans." *National Geographic.* August 29, 2015. www.nationalgeographic .com/science/article/150828-data-points-how-hurricane-katrina-changed-new-orleans.

Okazaki, Kenji, Krishna S. Pribadi, and Dyah Kusumastuti. "Learning on the Safety Issues of Reconstructed Houses from the 2004 Great Indian Ocean Earthquake and Tsunami in Aceh, Indonesia." In *Recovery from the Indian Ocean Tsunami: A Ten-Year Journey*, edited by Rajib Shaw. London: Springer, 2015, pp. 241–57.

Oliver-Smith, Anthony. "Haiti's 500-Year Earthquake." In *Tectonic Shifts: Haiti since the Earthquake*, edited by Mark Schuller and Pablo Morales. Sterling, VA: Kumarian Press, 2012, pp. 18–23.

Oliver-Smith, Anthony. "Introduction: Disaster Context and Causation: An Overview of Changing Perspectives in Disaster Research." In *Natural Disasters and Cultural Responses*, edited by Anthony Oliver-Smith. Williamsburg, VA: Department of Anthropology – College of William and Mary, 1986, pp. 1–34.

Oreskes, Naomi, and Erik M. Conway. *Merchants of Doubt: How a Handful of Scientists Obscured the Truth on Issues from Tobacco Smoke to Global Warming.* New York: Bloomsbury, 2010.

Oven, Katie, and Greg Bankoff. "The Neglected Country(side): Earthquake Risk Perceptions and Disaster Risk Reduction in Post-Soviet Rural Kazakhstan." *Journal of Rural Studies* 80 (2020): 171–84.

Patterson, Thom. "Katrina Evacuees Shift Houston's Identity." *CNN.* August 12, 2011. www.cnn.com/2011/US/08/12/katrina.houston/index.html.

Paul, Bimal Kanti. "Valdivia Earthquake, Chile, 1960." In *Natural Hazards and Disasters: From Avalanches and Climate Change to Water Spouts and Wildfires, V. 2*, edited by Bimal Kanti Paul. Santa Barbara, CA: ABC-CLIO, 2020, pp. 309–12.

Payton, Claire Antone. "Concrete Kleptocracy and Haiti's Culture of Building: Toward a New Temporality of Disaster." In *Critical Disaster Studies*, edited by Jacob A. C. Remes and Andy Horowitz. Philadelphia: University of Pennsylvania Press, 2021, pp. 71–84.

Pearce, Fred. "A Decade After Asian Tsunami, New Forests Protect the Coast." *Yale Environment 360*. December 4, 2014. https://e360.yale.edu/features/a_decade_after_asian_tsunami_new_forests_protect_the_coast.

Penn, Richard, Stanley Wild, Jorge Mascarenhas, and Jorge Mascarennas. "The Pombaline Quarter of Lisbon: An Eighteenth-Century Example of Prefabrication and Dimensional Co-ordination." *Construction History* 11 (1995): 3–17.

Plyer, Allison. "Population Shifts across Metro New Orleans." *The Data Center*. October 25, 2021. www.datacenterresearch.org/reports_analysis/population-shifts-across-metro-new-orleans.

Plyer, Allison. "What Census 2010 Reveals about Population and Housing in New Orleans and the Metro Area." *Greater New Orleans Community Data Center*. March 17, 2011. https://gnocdc.s3.amazonaws.com/reports/GNOCDC_Census2010PopulationAndHousing.pdf.

Pyne, Stephen J. *Fire: A Brief History*. Seattle: University of Washington Press, 2001.

Pyne, Stephen J. *Fire in America: A Cultural History of Wildland and Rural Fire*. Princeton, NJ: Princeton University Press, 1985.

Reiny, Samson. "NASA Study: First Direct Proof of Ozone Hole Recovery Due to Chemicals Ban." *NASA*. January 4, 2018. www.nasa.gov/feature/goddard/2018/nasa-study-first-direct-proof-of-ozone-hole-recovery-due-to-chemicals-ban.

Remes, Jacob A. C., and Andy Horowitz, editors. *Critical Disaster Studies*. Philadelphia: University of Pennsylvania Press, 2021.

Rodrigues, Lúcia Lima, and Russell Craig. "Recovery amid Destruction: Manoel Da Maya and the Lisbon Earthquake of 1755." *Libraries & the Cultural Record* 43, no. 4 (2008): 397–410.

Rosenberg, Charles E. *The Cholera Years: The United States in 1832, 1849, and 1866.* Chicago, IL: University of Chicago Press, 1962.

Rozario, Kevin. *The Culture of Calamity: Disaster and the Making of Modern America.* Chicago, IL: Chicago University Press, 2007.

Saatcioglu, M., A. Ghobarah, and I. Nistor. "Performance of Structures Affected by the 2004 Sumatra Tsunami in Thailand and Indonesia." In *The Indian Ocean Tsunami,* edited by Tad S. Murty, U. Aswathanarayana, and Niru Nirupama. London: CRC Press, 2007, pp. 297–321.

Sawislak, Karen. *Smoldering City: Chicagoans and the Great Fire, 1871–1874.* Chicago, IL: University of Chicago Press, 1995.

Schreurs, Miranda A. "Improving Governance Structures for Natural Disaster Response: Lessons from the Indian Ocean Tsunami." In *The Indian Ocean Tsunami: The Global Response to a Natural Disaster,* edited by Pradyumna P. Karan and Shanmugam Subbiah. Lexington: University Press of Kentucky, 2011, pp. 261–80.

Short, John Rennie, and Abbey Farmer. "Cities and Climate Change." *Earth 2* (2021): 1038–45.

Sisson, Patrick. "Puerto Rican Exodus to Central Florida Begs Question: Where's the Plan?" *Curbed.* December 19, 2017. https://archive.curbed .com/2017/12/19/16792936/hurricane-maria-puerto-rico-florida-orlando.

Smith, Carl. *Chicago's Great Fire: The Destruction and Resurrection of an Iconic American City.* New York: Grove Atlantic, 2020.

Snowden, Frank M. *Epidemics and Society: From the Black Death to the Present.* New Haven, CT: Yale University Press, 2019.

"Snowless Winters." *Saint Paul Daily Globe.* January 17, 1890.

Social Welfare History Project, VCU Libraries. "Tenement House Reform." *Social Welfare History Project.* 2018. https://socialwelfare.library.vcu.edu/ issues/poverty/tenement-house-reform.

Steinberg, Ted. *Acts of God: The Unnatural History of Natural Disaster in America.* New York: Oxford University Press, 2000.

Steinberg, Ted. "Afterword." *Environmental Disaster in the Gulf South: Two Centuries of Catastrophe, Risk, and Resilience,* edited by Cindy Ermus. Baton Rouge: Louisiana State University Press, 2018, pp. 184–94.

Stevens Crawshaw, Jane L. *Plague Hospitals: Public Health for the City in Early Modern Venice.* New York: Routledge, 2016.

Toledano, Roulhac. *A Pattern Book of New Orleans Architecture.* New Orleans, 2010.

Tomić, Zlata Blažina, and Vesna Blažina. *Expelling the Plague: The Health Office and the Implementation of Quarantine in Dubrovnik, 1377–1533.* Montreal: McGill-Queen's University Press, 2015.

Trouillot, Évelyne. "Eternity Lasted Less Than Sixty Seconds ..." In *Haitian Histories: New Perspectives*, edited by Alyssa Goldstein Sepinwall. New York: Routledge, 2013, pp. 312–16.

Umitsu, Masatomo. "The Tsunami Disaster on the Andaman Sea Coast of Thailand." In *The Indian Ocean Tsunami: The Global Response to a Natural Disaster*, edited by Pradyumna P. Karan and Shanmugam Subbiah. Lexington: University Press of Kentucky, 2011, pp. 35–50.

United Nations. "Cities: A 'Cause of and Solution to' Climate Change." *UN News*. September 18, 2019. https://news.un.org/en/story/2019/09/1046662.

United Nations. "Climate and Weather-Related Disasters Surge Five-Fold over 50 Years, but Early Warnings Save Lives: WMO Report." *UN News*. September 1, 2021. https://news.un.org/en/story/2021/09/1098662.

United Nations. "IPCC Report: 'Code Red' for Human Driven Global Heating, Warns UN Chief." *UN News*. August 9, 2021. https://news.un.org/en/story/2021/08/1097362.

United Nations. "The Ocean Conference Fact Sheet: People and Oceans." *UN Sustainable Development Goals*. New York: 2017. www.un.org/sustainable development/wp-content/uploads/2017/05/Ocean-fact-sheet-package.pdf.

United Nations, Department of Social and Economic Affairs, Population Division. *The World's Cities in 2018*. New York: United Nations, 2018.

United Nations Environmental Programme. "The Montreal Protocol." *UN Environment*. www.unep.org/ozonaction/who-we-are/about-montreal-protocol.

United Nations Office for Disaster Risk Reduction (UNDRR). "Build Back Better in Recovery, Rehabilitation and Reconstruction." Geneva: United Nations Office for Disaster Risk Reduction, 2017. www.undrr.org/files/53213_bbb.pdf.

United Nations Office for Disaster Risk Reduction (UNDRR). "Terminology." www.undrr.org/terminology.

United States Congress, House Committee on Science and Technology, Subcommittee on the Environment and the Atmosphere. *The National Climate Program Act: Hearings before the Subcommittee on the Environment and the Atmosphere of the Committee on Science and Technology, U.S. House of Representatives, Ninety-Fourth Congress*. Washington, DC: U.S. Government Printing Office, 1976.

United States Environmental Protection Agency, "Climate Change Indicators: Sea Level." *EPA.gov*. April 2021. www.epa.gov/climate-indicators/climate-change-indicators-sea-level.

United States Environmental Protection Agency, "Climate Change Indicators: Wildfires." *EPA.gov*. April 2021. www.epa.gov/climate-indicators/climate-change-indicators-wildfires#ref4.

Valle, Ariana. "¡Puerto Rico Se Levanta! Hurricane Maria and Narratives of Struggle, Resilience, and Migration." *Natural Hazards Center Quick Response Grant Report Series*, 279. Boulder: Natural Hazards Center, University of Colorado Boulder, 2018. https://hazards.colorado.edu/quick-response-report/puerto-rico-se-levanta-hurricane-maria-and-narratives-of-struggle-resilience-and-migration. https://hazards.colorado.edu/quick-response-report/puerto-rico-se-levanta-hurricane-maria-and-narratives-of-struggle-resilience-and-migration

Vazquez, Maegan. "San Juan Mayor Says the Trump Administration Killed Thousands through Neglect during Hurricane Maria." *CNN Politics*. August 29, 2018. www.cnn.com/2018/08/29/politics/san-juan-mayor-carmen-yulin-cruz-death-toll-cnntv/index.html.

Versluis, Anna. "Haiti Earthquake, 2010." In *Natural Hazards and Disasters: From Avalanches and Climate Change to Water Spouts and Wildfires, V. 2*, edited by Bimal Kanti Paul. Santa Barbara, CA: ABC-CLIO, 2020, pp. 137–41.

Weber, Melissa. "Rural Areas May Suffer Disproportionately in Quakes." *Temblor* (August 2020). http://doi.org/10.32858/temblor.113.

Wilson Jr., Samuel. *The Vieux Carré, New Orleans: Its Plan, Its Growth, Its Architecture* . . . New Orleans, LA: Bureau of Governmental Research, 1968.

Wu, Pei-Chin, Meng (Matt) Wei, and Steven D'Hondt. "Subsidence in Coastal Cities throughout the World Observed by InSAR." *Geophysical Research Letters* 49, no. 7 (April 2022): 1–11. https://agupubs.onlinelibrary.wiley.com/doi/10.1029/2022GL098477.

Wyss, Max. "Rural Populations Suffer Most in Great Earthquakes." *Seismological Research Letters* 89, no. 6 (2018): 1991–7.

Cambridge Elements ≡

Global Urban History

Michael Goebel

Graduate Institute Geneva

Michael Goebel is the Pierre du Bois Chair Europe and the World and Associate Professor of International History at the Graduate Institute Geneva. His research focuses on the histories of nationalism, of cities, and of migration. He is the author of *Anti-Imperial Metropolis: Interwar Paris and the Seeds of Third World Nationalism* (2015).

Tracy Neumann

Wayne State University

Tracy Neumann is an Associate Professor of History at Wayne State University. Her research focuses on global and transnational approaches to cities and the built environment. She is the author of *Remaking the Rust Belt: The Postindustrial Transformation of North America* (2016) and of essays on urban history and public policy.

Joseph Ben Prestel

Freie Universität Berlin

Joseph Ben Prestel is an Assistant Professor (wissenschaftlicher Mitarbeiter) of history at Free University of Berlin. His research focuses on the histories of Europe and the Middle East in the nineteenth and twentieth centuries as well as on global and urban history. He is the author of *Emotional Cities: Debates on Urban Change in Berlin and Cairo, 1860–1910* (2017).

About the Series

This series proposes a new understanding of urban history by reinterpreting the history of the world's cities. While urban history has tended to produce single-city case studies, global history has mostly been concerned with the interconnectedness of the world. Combining these two approaches produces a new framework to think about the urban past. The individual titles in the series emphasize global, comparative, and transnational approaches. They deliver empirical research about specific cities, while also exploring questions that expand the narrative outside the immediate locale to give insights into global trends and conceptual debates. Authored by established and emerging scholars whose work represents the most exciting new directions in urban history, this series makes pioneering research accessible to specialists and non-specialists alike.

Cambridge Elements ≡

Global Urban History